THE HOLY FACE

AND

THE LITTLE WAY

A Devotional Mission with

Fulton J. Sheen and

St. Thérèse of Lisieux

Allan Smith

Published by: Bishop Sheen Today

www.bishopsheentoday.com

Title: The Holy Face and the Little Way.   A Devotional Mission with Fulton J. Sheen and St. Thérèse of Lisieux.

Compiled by Allan J. Smith.   Includes bibliographical references.

Book formatting and design by Ajayi Isaac

mailto:smeplegacy@gmail.com/ +2348162435897

Identifiers:

ISBN (Paperback): 978-1-997627-58-6

ISBN (eBook): 978-1-997627-59-3

ISBN (Hardcover): 978-1-997627-60-9

Subjects: Jesus Christ — The Holy Hour — Prayer and Meditation – The Holy Face Devotion - St. Thérèse of Lisieux – Archbishop Fulton J. Sheen

THE HOLY FACE AND THE LITTLE WAY

A Devotional Mission with Fulton J. Sheen

and St. Thérèse of Lisieux.

A Sheen Mission Series - Volume I

The Sheen Mission Series invites you to walk with Archbishop Fulton J. Sheen in prayer, reparation, and renewal — a journey of the Holy Face, the Cross, the Eucharist and Our Blessed Mother.

Description:

The Holy Face and the Little Way is the first volume in the Sheen Mission Series — a prayerful journey inspired by the spirituality of Archbishop Fulton J. Sheen and St. Thérèse of Lisieux.

In these pages, you will discover how the "Little Way" of trust and love is united to the devotion of the Holy Face of Jesus. This treasury includes meditations, prayers, and reflections that will guide you into deeper union with Christ through adoration, reparation, and confidence in His merciful love.

Series Note:

This book is the first of four volumes in *The Sheen Mission Series*, a collection of spiritual companions for personal devotion and parish renewal:

1. **Volume II – *Behold Your Mother***
2. **Volume III – *The Cross and the Last Words***
3. **Volume IV – *Lord, Show Us Thy Face and We Shall Be Saved***

"One of the greatest tragedies in the world is wasted pain. Pain without relation to the Cross is like an unsigned check – without value. But once we have it countersigned with the Signature of the Saviour on the Cross, it takes on an infinite value."

— Archbishop Fulton J. Sheen

Dedication:

To Our Lady

of the

Holy Name of God

&

To the members of the

Archconfraternity

of the Holy Face,

both living and deceased

J M J

Archbishop Fulton J. Sheen gave us his mission statement in the opening lines of his 1949 New York Times best-selling book, *Peace of Soul*, with the words, "Unless Souls are saved, nothing is saved.

The purpose of this book is to continue Sheen's mission, pointing to the necessity of saving souls, especially our own.

Over the years, through presentations in parishes, conferences, radio broadcasts, and online, I have been blessed to share the life and works of the Venerable Archbishop Fulton J. Sheen, as well as the spirituality of St. Thérèse of the Child Jesus and the Holy Face. Their combined words of wisdom and practical spirituality hold a timeless appeal. In addition, the reader will also find many traditional Catholic devotional prayers.

The following are some of the aims for this devotional mission. First, to aid the reader in developing the virtue of piety by setting aside a time for daily prayer. Secondly, to promote devotion to our blessed Lord's Passion, specifically to His Holy Face. Thirdly, to further understand and come to practice St. Thérèse's *'Little Way'* of life.

It is my prayer that these pious reflections will quietly make their way into hospital rooms, adoration chapels, retreat centers, prison libraries, and to the bedside tables of the faithful and the lost, whereupon a soul, searching for the meaning of his or her life, will open its pages and find that all along, the merciful Christ was with them.

Archbishop Fulton J. Sheen once said that *"books are the most patient of teachers."* Hopefully, with time, this book will offer you some words of encouragement and some practical advice in advancing in the spiritual life.

Sit Nomen Domini Benedictum!

Blessed be the Name of the Lord!

Allan J. Smith

August 25, 2025

Feast of King St. Louis IX

Patron of the Archconfraternity of the Holy Face

x

Table of Contents

Foreword

There is a Face behind the silence of the Eucharist. A Face behind the veil of suffering. A Face behind the hiddenness of love. This book is an invitation to gaze upon that Face — the bruised, radiant, sorrowful, and saving Face of Christ.

Archbishop Fulton J. Sheen once said, 'The world's greatest need is to rediscover the true image of Christ's Face — a Face of mercy, not judgment; of tenderness, not wrath.' He believed that before we reform the world, we must first adore. And before we preach, we must first look — silently, lovingly — upon the Holy Face of Jesus.

In these pages, you will find a sacred meeting between the wisdom of Sheen and the heart of St. Thérèse of Lisieux. Two souls who, though separated by time and vocation, both found their mission in loving the Face of the Crucified One. St. Thérèse once wrote, 'Thy Face is my only wealth... I no longer ask for anything but love.' Fulton Sheen would echo her sentiment in his own way: 'It is not what we do for Christ that makes us holy — it is what we allow Him to do in us.

This book is not a theological treatise or a spiritual manual. It is a pilgrimage. A series of reflections, devotions, and meditations meant to draw you closer to the One who hides Himself in silence, and who reveals Himself in love.

May every page lead you to the Face of Christ. And may that Face — once looked upon — never be forgotten.

Introduction
Why the Holy Face? Why Now?

We live in an age of distractions. Noise fills our minds, screens occupy our attention, and our hearts often wander, numb from the weight of the world's demands. In the midst of this, the Holy Face of Christ calls us — quietly, insistently — to return. To remember. To behold.

Why the Holy Face? Because it is the most human part of Christ, and the most wounded. It is the part we spit upon in sin and the part we seek in sorrow. The Face reveals the Person. And the bruised Face of Jesus reveals the cost of love, the depth of mercy, and the grief of forgotten intimacy.

Why now? Because the world has forgotten how to blush. Archbishop Sheen wrote, 'The greatest loss of our time is the loss of the sense of sin.' And what restores it? A Face that suffers silently. A Face that absorbs hatred without retaliation. A Face that still looks upon us with love.

This devotion is not sentimental. It is not sweet. It is soul-rending. It asks us to look upon what we have done to Love — and to make reparation not out of guilt, but out of desire. Desire to console. Desire to remain. Desire to love more purely in a world that loves too little.

In these chapters, you will walk with Fulton Sheen and St. Thérèse. You will be invited to kneel, to look, and to let the Holy Face imprint itself upon your soul. And if you let it, you will never look at the Cross — or at another soul — the same way again.

Why the Holy Face? Why now? Because Christ is still asking, 'Who will stay with Me?' And the only worthy answer is the offering of your heart.

Chapter 1:
The Hidden Face of God and the Mission of Love

Archbishop Fulton Sheen often said that the greatest tragedy of modern times is not rebellion, but forgetfulness. We have not so much rejected God — we have simply ignored His Face.

He warned that when man loses the sense of sin, he loses the capacity to recognize the sacred. The Eucharist becomes a symbol. The Cross, a decoration. And the Face of Christ? Hidden behind the veil of indifference.

But St. Thérèse saw that Face. She called it "the only beauty that ravished my heart." And rather than run from it, she leaned in. She saw His bruises as invitations. His silence is speech. And she made of her life one long act of reparation.

Fulton Sheen was drawn to the mystery of reparation — that the greatest love we can show to God is not in words, but in willingly standing beside Him in silence, when others flee. This is what the saints did. This is what St. Thérèse did. This is what we are invited to do.

To contemplate the Holy Face of Christ is not just a private devotion. It is a mission. It is to become a Veronica in a world that spits and turns away — to wipe the Face of Christ by acts of love, adoration, sacrifice, and fidelity.

In this age of noise, distraction, and spiritual amnesia, we are called to remember the Face that loved us unto death. The bruised Face. The silent Face. The Holy Face.

This book is a pilgrimage with two great souls — Fulton Sheen and St. Thérèse — who beckon us toward that Face, not only to gaze upon it, but to carry its imprint into the world.

Let us begin — not with many words, but with hearts open to the Face of Love, hidden and holy.

Chapter 2:
St. Thérèse and the Offering of the Face

In the cloistered silence of Lisieux, a young Carmelite nun once knelt before a simple image: the Holy Face of Jesus. It was not majestic. It was not beautiful by worldly standards. It was bruised, spat upon, and crowned with thorns.

Yet St. Thérèse of the Child Jesus saw in that disfigured face the deepest truth of God's love — a love that hides itself, suffers silently, and offers itself without complaint.

Long before she would consecrate herself to Merciful Love, St. Thérèse gave herself to the Face of Christ. She joined the Archconfraternity of the Holy Face and even added the title 'of the Holy Face' to her religious name. This was not pious decoration — it was identity. It was a mission. It was her way of standing beside the Suffering Servant when so many turned away.

For St. Thérèse, the Holy Face was not a separate devotion; it was the very heart of her Little Way. She believed that to console Jesus in His hidden sufferings was the greatest act of love. And she did it not with grand acts or public witness, but with the offering of small things — accepted in silence, embraced in love, given without seeking praise.

Each annoyance, each trial, each moment of dryness in prayer became for her a veil lifted — an opportunity to see and kiss the wounds of Christ. She would say, 'I want to love Jesus so much, to console Him so much, that He will be forced to do my will — by doing His!'

And what was His will? That she should love Him in littleness, serve Him in obscurity, and console Him in His agony — not with words, but with trust.

To walk with St. Thérèse is to discover that the bruised Face of Christ is not a place of fear, but of encounter. It is where saints are born, and where sinners find mercy. It is where the mission of love begins.

Chapter 3:
Reparation and the Radiance
of the Hidden Christ

Reparation. It is a word that sounds severe to modern ears. Yet it is the language of love — not the love of sentiment, but of sacrifice. To make reparation is to offer something back to God, not because He needs it, but because we have wounded what is most beautiful: His love.

Fulton Sheen once said that we do not hate God; we simply forget Him. That is the great crime of the modern age — not defiance, but indifference. The Face of Christ is no longer rejected with fists, but ignored with shrugs. And so the Church, like Veronica, is called not to argue but to console.

Reparation begins in the heart. It is the silent 'I'm sorry' whispered before the Blessed Sacrament. It is the soul who kneels in a dark chapel while the world spins on in noise. It is the mother who offers her sleepless night, the priest who offers his hidden suffering, the child who accepts a small humiliation with love.

St. Thérèse understood that reparation was not about grand gestures, but about the quiet giving of self in union with Christ. She did not seek to escape suffering, but to infuse it with purpose. Every cough, every dryness in prayer, every misunderstanding — she kissed them like the bruises on His Face.

Fulton Sheen echoed this when he wrote, 'The greatest love is not to proclaim Christ but to suffer with Him.' In this way, reparation becomes radiant. It is not bitter; it is beautiful. It does not draw attention to itself, but to Him. It restores what sin disfigures — not with vengeance, but with love.

In contemplating the Holy Face, we are drawn into this divine exchange. We see not just what sin has done to God, but what love has done for us. We gaze upon His wounds and discover our mission: to return love for love, silence for mockery, fidelity for betrayal.

This is reparation: the radiant response of a soul who sees the Face of Christ and refuses to turn away.

Chapter 4:
The Holy Hour and the Veronica Vocation

In the Stations of the Cross, there is one encounter that stands out not for its drama, but for its intimacy: Veronica steps forward, breaks through the crowd, and wipes the Face of Jesus. She says nothing. She makes no speech. But her veil absorbs the blood and sweat of the Saviour, and her act becomes a Gospel of its own.

Archbishop Fulton Sheen often reflected on this moment. To him, Veronica represented every soul who dares to console Christ in a world that crucifies Him daily. Her gesture was reparation — not with sermons, but with tenderness, not with power, but with presence.

The Holy Hour, as Sheen practiced and preached it, is our way of becoming Veronica. When we kneel before the Eucharistic Christ, we are not merely fulfilling a devotion — we are wiping His Face. We are telling Him, with our silence and stillness, that He is not forgotten.

Fulton Sheen called the Holy Hour a 'daily hour of companionship with Christ.' He urged priests and laypeople alike to spend sixty minutes each day with the

Eucharistic Lord. Not for results, not for mystical experiences, but for love. For fidelity. For reparation.

St. Thérèse lived her Holy Hours in the hidden cloister of Lisieux. She had no chapel of exposition, no public platform. But she made of her duties, her prayers, and her little sacrifices a perpetual Holy Hour of the heart. She was a Veronica in silence, in sickness, in surrender.

To be a Veronica today is to go against the grain. It is to pause when others rush, to adore when others ignore, to enter the chapel when the world beckons us to scroll and scatter. But it is also to discover a beauty beyond words — the beauty of the Face of Christ etched upon our soul.

Let us enter the Holy Hour not as spectators, but as lovers. Let us become Veronicas. And let us never leave the Face of Christ untouched by our love.

Chapter 5:
The Little Way of Reparation

St. Thérèse once wrote, 'I have always wanted to be a saint… but I have always felt that I was incapable of great deeds.' It was this very awareness — her littleness — that led her to discover the path now known around the world as the Little Way.

The Little Way is not about doing less. It is about doing with greater love. It is about doing the unnoticed, the uncelebrated, the mundane — with the heart of one who knows Christ is watching.

For St. Thérèse, the Little Way became a school of reparation. She embraced daily annoyances, hidden sufferings, and acts of obedience as offerings to the Holy Face. Each small surrender became a kiss upon the bruises of Christ's love.

She understood that she could not ascend the mountain of perfection by her own strength. Instead, she would let Jesus lift her, like a child reaching upward with empty hands. Her smallness became her strength. Her weakness, her offering.

Archbishop Fulton Sheen echoed this when he wrote that sanctity is not about doing great things for God, but doing small things with great fidelity to His will. Reparation, he taught, begins with the acceptance of the present moment — without complaint, without spectacle, without applause.

In a world obsessed with results, St. Thérèse teaches us that love does not measure itself by success. It measures itself by surrender. It is not how much we do, but how much we yield — how much we allow ourselves to be poured out in silence, for love alone.

The Little Way is not an escape from the cross; it is a hidden path into its heart. It is there, on the narrow road of daily sacrifice, that the Holy Face shines — not in majesty, but in mercy.

Let us walk this way. Let us make our lives a mosaic of hidden offerings. Let us become saints — not by great deeds, but by great love.

Chapter 6:
The Consoling Gaze

There is a kind of healing that happens not through words, but through gaze. A glance that understands. A look that listens. In the spiritual life, it is not always what we say to God that matters most — it is how we allow ourselves to be seen by Him.

St. Thérèse often wrote about looking upon the Face of Jesus. For her, it was not an image to admire, but a place to rest. A sanctuary for her soul. She did not need to explain herself in prayer. She simply placed herself before Him — silent, still, and seen.

Fulton Sheen understood this, too. His Holy Hours were less about speaking and more about gazing — fixing his eyes on the Eucharist until the gaze of Christ began to change him. He called it 'radiation therapy for the soul.' We become what we behold.

In a world that stares but does not see, the Holy Face calls us back to the power of presence. In Adoration, we come not to perform, but to console. We let the eyes of Christ meet our wounds. We let His silence absorb our noise. We allow His gaze to say what words cannot.

Reparation is born in this gaze. When we behold the disfigured Face of Christ and still find beauty, we begin to see as God sees. We begin to recognize the value of souls, the dignity of suffering, and the hiddenness of grace.

St. Thérèse believed that just one glance of love toward the Face of Christ could change a heart, lift a soul, and bring consolation to a God so often forgotten. She gave Him her gaze — not once, but daily. In doing so, she received His peace.

Let us return our gaze to Christ. Let us adore Him with the eyes of the heart. And let us never forget that in every Holy Hour, He gazes back.

Chapter 7:
The Interior Life and the Hidden Christ

The world today is noisy. Its rhythms are rushed, its values external, and its heroes often loud. But the saints teach us that holiness grows in silence. Intimacy with God is not born in the glare of applause, but in the quiet of the interior life.

St. Thérèse lived almost her entire vocation in obscurity. Her greatness was not seen, not praised, not published — until after her death. She was hidden, like the Eucharist. And it was there, in that hiddenness, that her intimacy with Christ deepened beyond words.

Fulton Sheen emphasized again and again that the strength of a priest, of a layperson, of the Church itself, depends on the interior life. He wrote, 'The future of the world and of the Church passes through the family and through the interior life of its members.' This interior life — rooted in prayer, silence, and self-gift — is the soil of sanctity.

The Holy Face devotion is a direct invitation into the interior life. We are not asked to do something dramatic, but to look deeply, silently, reverently. To behold the Face of Christ is to begin a conversation of the soul, a love that grows wordlessly in the heart's sanctuary.

Reparation begins here. Not in public penance, but in hidden offerings. Not in declarations, but in desires. The desire to love, to repair, to remain — even when unseen, even when unthanked. Especially then.

St. Thérèse knew that interior silence was the womb of divine action. She said, 'My vocation is love.' And love, she knew, is most fruitful when it is most free of self.

Let us cultivate this interior garden — not with striving, but with surrender. Let us meet the hidden Christ with hidden hearts. And there, in the silence, let the Holy Face become the mirror in which we are formed anew.

Chapter 8:
The Cross and the Countenance of Mercy

The Holy Face of Jesus is inseparable from the Cross. It is there, on Calvary, that the Face is most revealed — bruised, broken, and yet radiant with mercy.

St. Thérèse wrote, 'It is through suffering that I have come to love the Cross.' She understood that the Cross was not a contradiction of God's love, but its most eloquent expression. To love the Face of Christ is to accept the shadow of the Cross, not as punishment, but as participation.

Fulton Sheen, too, placed the Cross at the center of the spiritual life. He saw in the Passion not only the redemption of man, but the unveiling of the divine heart. He said, 'Unless there is a Good Friday in your life, there can be no Easter Sunday.

The Countenance of Christ crucified is not a face of defeat. It is the Face of mercy, poured out. Every wound becomes a word, every drop of blood a prayer, every silence an act of surrender.

To contemplate the Holy Face is to enter into the Paschal Mystery — to unite our sufferings with His, to offer our lives in reparation, and to be transformed by love that does not flee from the Cross.

St. Thérèse did not seek suffering, but she did not run from it. She saw it as her way to love more, to console Jesus more, to become more like Him. And through that suffering, she radiated joy — not superficial cheer, but the deep peace of a soul resting in the will of God.

We, too, are called to let the Cross etch itself onto our hearts. Not as a burden alone, but as a blessing. Not as death, but as a door.

Let us lift our gaze to the Holy Face on the Cross. Let it teach us what love looks like when it is poured out. And let our lives become a reflection of that Countenance — a mirror of mercy in a world in need of hope.

Chapter 9:
Love Alone Remains

There comes a point on the spiritual path when everything else falls away — the consolations, the clarity, even the strength we once felt. What remains is love. Love, not as a feeling, but as a decision. Love, not as fireworks, but as faithfulness.

St. Thérèse knew this well. Her final months were marked by darkness, dryness, and even doubt. Yet she chose to love. She smiled through her sufferings. She prayed when she felt nothing. She offered everything to Jesus with empty hands, saying, 'I choose all!'

Fulton Sheen taught that sanctity is not measured by visions or miracles, but by how much we allow Christ to live in us. He wrote, 'Christ is not loved because He is not known; and He is not known because His Face is not looked upon.' St. Thérèse looked — and she loved, even when that Face seemed hidden.

To love in darkness is the highest act of faith. To say, 'Though He slay me, yet will I trust in Him,' is to echo the words of Job and the soul of St. Thérèse. It is to become reparation not just in action, but in being.

The Holy Face calls us to this surrender. To love for the sake of love. To remain faithful when everything else fades. To become, like Veronica and St. Thérèse, a resting place for Christ in a world of rejection.

When all is stripped away, love remains. And if we choose to remain in love, we remain in Him. That is the Little Way. That is the mystery of the Holy Face. That is the path of saints.

Let us end where we began — with a glance toward the Face of Christ. Let that glance become a gaze. Let that gaze become a gift. And let our hearts, like St. Thérèse's, whisper even in silence: 'My vocation is love.'

Chapter 10:
A Mission of Reparation

The journey does not end at the feet of Christ — it begins there. Having contemplated His Holy Face, having walked the path of silence, suffering, and surrender, we now rise to carry that Face into the world.

Reparation is not only a devotion; it is a mission. The bruises we have kissed in Adoration now appear on the faces of the forgotten. The silence we have kept with Christ is now needed in a world drowning in noise.

St. Thérèse once said, 'I would spend my heaven doing good on earth.' Her Little Way did not end in the cloister; it radiated outward. It became a light for missionaries, parents, priests, and ordinary souls who long to love heroically in hidden ways.

Fulton Sheen challenged every Christian to be an apostle of the Holy Hour, a consoler of Christ, and a mirror of His mercy. He believed reparation would renew the Church, not through programs or platforms, but through saints who kneel, adore, and offer.

You are part of this mission now. Your glance, your silence, your hidden act of love — these are not forgotten. They rise like incense before the throne of God. They wipe the Face of Christ in places where His Name is ignored and His love refused.

To live this mission is not to do more — it is to love more. To be available to grace. To be faithful in small things. To adore, to suffer, to rejoice — with Christ, for souls, in secret.

The Holy Face is not just a devotion to admire. It is a calling to answer. It is Christ, looking at you with eyes that say, 'Will you stay with Me?'

Let your answer be the life you live. Let your yes be daily. And let your heart, like St. Thérèse and Fulton Sheen, become a living veil — a place where the Holy Face finds rest, and the world finds hope.

Chapter 11:

Quotes from St. Thérèse of Lisieux and Archbishop Fulton J. Sheen

Quotes from St. Thérèse of Lisieux

"Thy Face is my only wealth. I ask nothing more."

"Jesus, Your Face is the only homeland of my heart."

"To live of love is to dry Your Face, to console You every hour of the day."

"I want to spend my heaven doing good on earth."

"I choose all! I want everything that Jesus wills for me."

"It is confidence and nothing but confidence that must lead us to Love."

"Suffering is the very best gift He has to give us. He gives it only to His chosen friends."

"I am not afraid of the darkness. My God, may Your Face shine on me only for a moment... and I shall be saved."

Quotes from Archbishop Fulton J. Sheen

"Christ is not loved because He is not known; and He is not known because His Face is not looked upon."

"Unless there is a Good Friday in your life, there can be no Easter Sunday."

"The greatest love story of all time is contained in a tiny white Host."

"The world's greatest need is to rediscover the true image of Christ's Face — a Face of mercy, not judgment; of tenderness, not wrath."

"The modern man has everything — except self-knowledge and God-awareness."

"We become like that which we gaze upon. Looking into a sunset, the face takes on a golden glow. Looking at the Holy Face of Christ, the soul does likewise."

"You must remember to love people and use things, rather than to love things and use people."

"The Holy Hour becomes like an oxygen tank to revive the breath of the Holy Spirit in the midst of the foul atmosphere of the world."

Chapter 12:
Scripture for Holy Hour Reflection

These Scripture passages have been selected to deepen one's meditation during a Holy Hour. They focus on the themes of the Holy Face, suffering, reparation, love, silence, and intimacy with God.

Psalm 27:8 – "Of you my heart has spoken: 'Seek his face.' It is your face, O Lord, that I seek."

Psalm 31:16 – "Let your face shine upon your servant; save me in your merciful love."

Psalm 80:3 – "Restore us, O God; let your face shine, that we may be saved."

Isaiah 53:2–5 – "He had no form or majesty that we should look at him, no beauty that we should desire him… He was despised and rejected by men; a man of sorrows… by his wounds we are healed."

Lamentations 3:28 – "Let him sit alone in silence when it is laid upon him."

Daniel 9:17 – "Now therefore, O our God, listen to the prayer of your servant… and cause your face to shine upon your sanctuary."

Matthew 26:38–40 – "Could you not watch one hour with me?"

Luke 22:61 – "The Lord turned and looked at Peter… and he went out and wept bitterly."

John 14:9 – "Whoever has seen me has seen the Father."

John 19:5 – "Jesus came out, wearing the crown of thorns and the purple robe. Pilate said to them, 'Behold the man!'"

2 Corinthians 4:6 – "God… has shone in our hearts to give the light of the knowledge of the glory of God in the face of Christ."

Hebrews 12:2–3 – "Looking to Jesus, the pioneer and perfecter of our faith… who endured the cross, despising the shame… Consider him who endured from sinners such hostility against himself, so that you may not grow weary or fainthearted."

Chapter 13:
How to Begin Your Own
Holy Hour of Reparation

The Holy Hour is not just a pious tradition — it is a powerful act of love and reparation. Archbishop Fulton J. Sheen called it 'the hour that makes the day holy.' St. Thérèse of Lisieux lived her own Holy Hours hidden in the cloister, offering little things with great love. The invitation is now extended to you.

Whether you are able to spend time before the Blessed Sacrament in a chapel or pray from home in spiritual communion, you can begin your own Holy Hour of Reparation with simple steps, intentional love, and quiet fidelity.

Suggested Structure for a Holy Hour

1. Begin with Silence (5 minutes) – Gaze upon the Holy Face of Christ. Ask for the grace to see Him in His sorrow, His silence, and His love.
2. Act of Contrition – Offer reparation for your sins and the sins of the world. You may pray: "O my Jesus, I am sorry for having offended You. I desire to console Your Heart."

3. Meditate on Scripture (10–15 minutes) – Choose one passage from the appendix or another Gospel scene. Let the words enter slowly. Listen.
4. Spiritual Reading (optional) – Read a short meditation or quote from St. Thérèse or Fulton Sheen. Let it echo silently in your heart.
5. Rosary or Chaplet of the Holy Face – Offer one of the prayers of reparation. Unite your intercessions to the wounds of Christ.
6. Quiet Adoration or Gaze (15 minutes) – Simply remain with Him. No need for many words. Be present. Be still. Be His.
7. Closing Prayer of Surrender – Offer a final prayer: "Jesus, may I never turn away from Your Face. Receive my heart as a veil of love and reparation."

Remember:

Your fidelity is more important than your feelings. A short, sincere Holy Hour done with love consoles Christ far more than lengthy words spoken without the heart. Begin where you are. Offer what you have. He will do the rest.

Chapter 14:
Fulton Sheen's Holy Hour Reflections

Why Make a Holy Hour

The purpose of these meditations is to aid souls in securing an inner peace by meditating for one continuous hour a day on God and our immortal destiny. Whether or not one uses these meditations does not matter in the least. Some Jews, some Protestants, and some Catholics may find it very unsatisfactory. If, however, they reject these because they wish to make the Holy Hour in their own way, they will have achieved its purpose. What is vital is not that these meditations be used, but that there be meditation.

But why spend an hour a day in meditation? Because we are living on the surface of our souls, knowing little of either God or our inner self. Our knowledge is mostly about things, not about destiny. Most of our difficulties and disappointments in life are due to mistakes in our life plans. Having forgotten the purpose of living, we have doubted even the value of living. A broken bone gives pain because it is not where it ought to be; our souls are in agony because we are not tending to the fullness of Life, Truth, and Love, which is God.

But Why Make a Holy Hour?
Here are Ten Reasons.

1. Because it is time spent in the Presence of Our Lord Himself, if faith is alive, no further reason is needed.

2. Because in our busy life, it takes considerable time to shake off the "noonday devils," the worldly cares, which cling to our souls, like dust. An hour with Our Lord follows the experience of the disciples on the road to Emmaus (Luke 24:13-35). We begin by walking with Our Lord, but our eyes are "held fast" so that we do not "recognize him". Next, He converses with our soul as we read the Scriptures. The third stage is one of sweet intimacy, as when 'he sat down at the table with them.' The fourth stage is the full dawning of the mystery of the Eucharist. Our eyes are "opened," and we recognize Him. Finally, we reach the point where we do not want to leave. The hour seemed so short. As we arise, we ask:

   Weren't our hearts burning within us when he spoke to us on the road, and when he made the Scriptures plain to us? (Luke 24:32)

3. Because Our Lord asked for it.

   Had you no strength, then, to watch with me even for an hour? (Matt. 26:40)

   The word was addressed to Peter, but he is referred to as Simon. It is our Simon-nature which needs the hour. If the hour seems hard, it is because … the spirit is willing enough, but the flesh is weak. (Mark 14:39)

4. Because the Holy Hour keeps a balance between the spiritual and the practical. Western philosophies tend to an activism in which God does nothing, and man everything; the Eastern philosophies tend to a quietism in which God does everything, and man nothing. The golden mean is in the words of St. Thomas: "action following rest," Martha walking with Mary. The Holy Hour unites the contemplative to the active life of the person.

   Thanks to the hour with Our Lord, our meditations and resolutions pass from the conscious to the subconscious and then become motives of action. A new spirit begins to pervade our work. The change is effected by Our Lord, Who fills our heart and works through our hands. A person can give only what he possesses. To give Christ to others, one must possess Him.

5. Because the Holy Hour will make us practice what we preach.

    Here is an image, he said, of the kingdom of heaven; there was once a king, who held a marriage feast for his son, and sent out his servants with a summons to all those whom he had invited to the wedding; but they would not come. (Matt. 22:2, 3)

    It was written of Our Lord that He 'set out to do and to teach' (Acts 1:1). The person who practices the Holy Hour will find that when he teaches, the people will say of him as of the Lord:

    All ... were astonished at the gracious words which came from his mouth. (Luke 4:22)

6. Because the Holy Hour helps us make reparation both for the sins of the world and for our own. When the Sacred Heart appeared to St. Margaret Mary, it was His Heart, and not His Head, that was crowned with thorns. It was Love that was hurt. Black Masses, sacrilegious communions, scandals, militant atheism – who will make up for them? Who will be an Abraham for Sodom, a Mary for those who have no wine? The sins of the world are our sins as if we had committed them. If they caused Our Lord a bloody sweat, to the point that

He upbraided His disciples for failing to stay with Him an hour, shall we with Cain ask:

Is it for me to watch over my brother?   (Gen. 4:9)

7. Because it reduces our liability to temptation and weakness. Presenting ourselves before Our Lord in the Blessed Sacrament is like putting a tubercular patient in good air and sunlight. The virus of our sins cannot long exist in the face of the Light of the world.

Always I can keep the Lord within sight; always he is at my right hand, to make me stand firm. (Psalm 15:8)

Our sinful impulses are prevented from arising through the barrier erected each day by the Holy Hour. Our will becomes disposed to goodness with little conscious effort on our part. Satan, the roaring lion, was not permitted to put forth his hand to touch righteous Job until he received permission (Job 1:12). Certainly then will the Lord withhold serious fall from him who watches (1 Cor. 10:13). With full confidence in his Eucharistic Lord, the person will have a spiritual resiliency. He will bounce back quickly after a falling: Fall I, it is but to rise again, sit I in darkness, the Lord will be my light. The Lord's displeasure I must bear, I that have sinned against him, till at last, he admits my plea, and grants redress. (Micah 7:8, 9)

The Lord will be favourable even to the weakest of us if He finds us at His feet in adoration, disposing ourselves to receive Divine favours. No sooner had Saul of Tarsus, the persecutor, humbled himself before his Maker than God sent a special messenger to his relief, telling him that 'even now he is at his prayers' (Acts 9:11). Even the person who has fallen can expect reassurance if he watches and prays.

They shall increase, that hitherto had dwindled, be exalted, that once were brought low. (Jer. 30:19, 20)

8. Because the Holy Hour is a personal prayer, the person who limits himself strictly to his official obligation is like the union man who downs tools the moment the whistle blows. Love begins when duty finishes. It is a giving of the cloak when the coat is taken. It is walking the extra mile.

Answer shall come ere cry for help is uttered; prayer find audience while it is yet on their lips. (Isa. 65:24)

Of course, we do not have to make a Holy Hour – and that is just the point. Love is never compelled, exccpt in hell. Their love has to submit to justice.

To be forced to love would be a kind of hell. No man who loves a woman is obligated to give her an engagement ring, and no person who loves the Sacred Heart ever has to give an engagement Hour.

"Would you, too, go away?" (John 6:68) is weak love; "Art thou sleeping?" (Mark 14:37) is irresponsible love; "He had great possessions" (Matt. 19:22; Mark 10:22) is selfish love. But does the person who loves His Lord have time for other activities before he performs acts of love "above and beyond the call of duty"? Does the patient love the physician who charges for every call, or does he begin to love when the physician says, "I just dropped by to see how you were"?

9. Meditation keeps us from seeking an external escape from our worries and miseries. When difficulties arise, when nerves are made taut by false accusations, there is always a danger that we may look outwards, as the Israelites did, for release.

From the Lord God, the Holy One of Israel, word was given to you, Come back and keep still, and all shall be well with you; in quietness and in confidence lies your strength. But you would have none of it; To horse! You cried We must flee! And flee you shall; We must ride swiftly, you said, but swifter still ride your pursuers. (Isa. 30:15, 16)

No outward escape, neither pleasure, drink, friends, nor keeping busy, is an answer. The soul cannot "fly upon a horse"; it must take "wings" to a place where its "life is hidden away ... with Christ in God" (Col. 3:3).

10. Finally, because the Holy Hour is necessary for the Church. No one can read the Old Testament without becoming conscious of the presence of God in history. How often did God use other nations to punish Israel for her sins? He made Assyria the "rod that executes my vengeance" (Isa.. 10:5). The history of the world since the Incarnation is the Way of the Cross. The rise of nations and their fall remain related to the Kingdom of God. We cannot understand the mystery of God's government, for it is the "sealed book" of the Apocalypse. John wept when he saw it (Rev. 5:4). He could not understand why this moment of prosperity and that hour of adversity.

The sole requirement is the venture of faith, and the reward is the depths of intimacy for those who cultivate His friendship. To abide with Christ is spiritual fellowship, as He insisted on the solemn and sacred night of the Last Supper, the moment He chose to give us the Eucharist:

You have only to live on in me, and I will live on in you. (John 15:4)

He wants us in His dwelling: That you, too, may be where I am. (John 14:3)

How to Make a Holy Hour

"Let nothing hinder thee from praying always and be not afraid to be justified even to death for the rewards of God continue forever. Before prayer prepare thy soul; and be not as a man that tempt God" (Sir. 18; 22-23).

Prayer is the lifting of our soul to God, unto the end of perfectly corresponding to His Holy Will. Our Divine Lord, describing His Mission, said: "For I have come down from heaven, not to do my own will, but the will of him who sent me ... the Father, that I should lose nothing of what he has given me, but that I should raise it up on the last day" (John 6:38, 39). "My food is to do the will of him who sent me, to accomplish his work" (John 4:34).

To correspond to the Divine Will, we must, first of all, know it, and secondly, have the grace and strength to correspond with it, once it is known. But to attain these two gifts of light for our minds and power for our wills, we must live on terms of intimate friendship with God. This is done through prayer. A prayerful life is, therefore, one lived in conformity with the Holy Will of God, as a prayerless life is a life of self-will and selfishness.

There is an element of prayer common to Jews, Protestants, and Catholics, namely, belief in God. Above half of the prayers, for example, which a priest says in his Divine Office, are taken from the Old Testament. In relation to all three, that is, Jews, Protestants, and Catholics, a Holy Hour will, therefore, be understood as one Hour a day spent in meditating on God and our eternal salvation. This Holy Hour can be made anywhere.

For Catholics, however, the Holy Hour has a very special significance. It means a continuous and unbroken Hour spent in the presence of Our Divine Lord in the Eucharist; for which reason, a meditation on the Blessed Eucharist has been included as one of these meditations in this book.

In the case of priests and religious, it is suggested that they make this Holy Hour in addition to their usual recitation of the Divine Office and Holy Mass.

This Holy Hour will be spent in prayer and meditation. A distinction is here made between the two, with the emphasis on the latter. By prayer, we here understand the recitation of formal prayers, generally composed by a person different from him who prays.

The Psalms represent one of the highest forms of vocal prayer and are common to Jews, Protestants, and Catholics. Other vocal prayers include the Our Father, Hail Mary, Creed, Confiteor, Acts of Faith, Hope, and Charity, and thousands of other prayers found in religious books. There are three kinds of attention in vocal prayer: (1) to the words, lest we say them wrong; (2) to their sense and meaning; and (3) to God and the intention for which we pray. The last kind of attention is essential to vocal prayer.

But the principal purpose of these Holy Hour meditations is the cultivation of mental prayer or meditation. Very few souls ever meditate; they are either frightened by the word or else never taught its existence. In the human order, a person in love is always conscious of the one loved, lives in the presence of the other, resolves to do the will of the other, and regards as his greatest jealousy being outdone in the least advantage of self-giving. Apply this to a soul in love with God, and you have the rudiments of meditation.

Meditation is, therefore, a kind of communing of spirit with spirit, with God as its object. Without attempting to set down the formal aspects of meditation, but to make it as intelligible as possible to beginners, the technique of meditation is as follows:

1. We speak to God: We begin by putting ourselves in the presence of God. For those who make the Holy Hour before the Blessed Sacrament, there must be a consciousness of our presence before the Body, Blood, Soul, and Divinity of Our Lord and Saviour Jesus Christ. Naturally, there are varying degrees of intimacy with persons. In a theatre, there are hundreds present, but little or no intimacy between them. The intimacy deepens to

the degree that we establish conversation with one or more of them, and according as this conversation springs from a common interest. So it is with God.

Prayer, then, is not a mere asking for things, but an aiming at a transformation; that is, a becoming "conformed to the image of his Son" (Rom. 8:29). We pray not to dispose God to give us something, but to dispose ourselves to receive something from Him: the fullness of Divine Life.

2. God speaks to us: Activity is not only on the human side but also on the Divine. A conversation is an exchange, not a monologue. As the soul willed to draw near God, God wills to draw near the soul. It would be wrong to monopolize the conversation with friends; it is more wrong to do so in our relations with God. We must not do all the talking; we must also be good listeners. "Speak Lord, for thy servant heareth" (1 Kings 3:9).

The soul now experiences the truth of the words "Draw near to God, and he will draw near to you" (James 4:8) All during the meditation, it will conceive devout affections of adoration, petition, sacrifice, and reparation to God, but particularly at the close of the meditation. These affections or colloquies are to be offered preferably in our own language, for every soul must make its own love to God, and God loves each soul in a particular manner.

"In the beginning, the soul attracted to Jesus by some impulse of grace comes to Him, filled with natural thoughts and aspirations, and very ignorant of the supernatural. It understands neither God nor itself. It has a few intimate relations with the Divinity outside of itself and within itself, but it begins to converse with Jesus. If it persists in the frequentation of His company, the Lord gradually takes an ever-increasing share in the conversation and begins to enlighten the soul.

In its contemplation of the mysteries of faith, He aids it to penetrate beneath the words and facts and symbols, hitherto known but superficially, and to grasp the inner sense of the supernatural truths contained in these facts or words or symbols. The Scriptures are gradually opened to the soul. The well-known texts begin to acquire a new and deeper meaning. Familiar expressions convey a knowledge, which the soul wonders never to have before discovered in them. All this new light is directed towards giving a fuller and more perfect comprehension of the mysteries of our faith, which are the mysteries of the life of Jesus" (Leen, Progress Through Mental Prayer, p. 29. Sheed & Ward).

Do not read these meditations as a story. Read a few lines slowly; close the book; think about the truth contained in them; apply them to your own life; speak to God about how little you have corresponded to His Will, how anxious you are to do it; listen to God speaking to your soul; make acts of faith, hope, and love to God, and only when that train of thought has been exhausted should you proceed to the next idea. A single Holy Hour will not necessarily require reading a chapter of this book. If one meditates well, a single chapter should provide thoughts for many Holy Hours.

When this book of meditations is exhausted, take up either the Sacred Scriptures or some truly spiritual book, or the life of a saint, and use it for inspiration and for meditation.

Appendix I:
Prayers of the Holy Face Devotion

The prayers and devotions contained in Appendices I–VI are taken, either wholly or in part, from the *Manual of the Archconfraternity of the Holy Face* (1887), compiled by the Reverend Abbé Janvier. They are reproduced here in their traditional form so that readers today may continue to participate in the same acts of reparation, adoration, and love practiced by generations of the faithful devoted to the Holy Face of Our Blessed Lord.

The Little
Chaplet
of the Holy Face

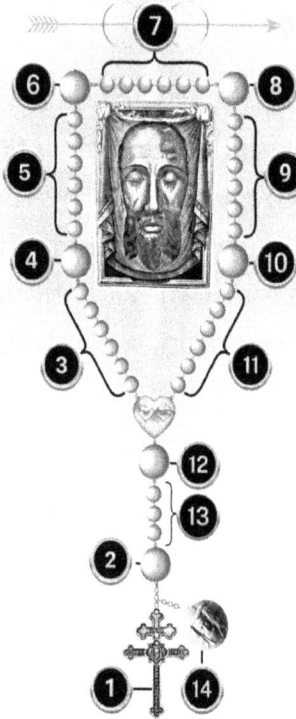

1

On the Crucifix make the sign of the Cross.

O God, come to my assistance; O Lord make haste to help me. Glory be to the Father and to the Son and to the Holy Ghost. As it was in the beginning, is now, and ever shall be, world without end. Amen.

2

My Jesus, Mercy. In honour of the sense of Touch.

Glory be to the Father and to the Son and to the Holy Ghost. As it was in the beginning, is now, and ever shall be, world without end. Amen.

3

Arise, O Lord, and let Thine enemies be scattered, and let them that hate Thee flee from before Thy Face. (X6)

4

My Jesus, Mercy. In honour of the sense of Hearing.

Glory be to the Father and to the Son and to the Holy Ghost. As it was in the beginning, is now, and ever shall be, world without end. Amen.

5

Arise, O Lord, and let Thine enemies be scattered, and let them that hate Thee flee from before Thy Face. (X6)

6

My Jesus, Mercy. In honour of the sense of Sight.

Glory be to the Father and to the Son and to the Holy Ghost. As it was in the beginning, is now, and ever shall be, world without end. Amen.

7

Arise, O Lord, and let Thine enemies be scattered, and let them that hate Thee flee from before Thy Face. (X6)

8

My Jesus, Mercy. In honour of the sense of Smell.

Glory be to the Father and to the Son and to the Holy Ghost. As it was in the beginning, is now, and ever shall be, world without end. Amen.

9

Arise, O Lord, and let Thine enemies be scattered, and let them that hate Thee flee from before Thy Face. (X6)

10

My Jesus, Mercy. In honour of the sense of Taste.

Glory be to the Father and to the Son and to the Holy Ghost. As it was in the beginning, is now, and ever shall be, world without end. Amen.

11

Arise, O Lord, and let Thine enemies be scattered, and let them that hate Thee flee from before Thy Face. (X6)

12

My Jesus, Mercy. Let us recall to mind the public life of the Saviour and let us honour all the wounds of His adorable Face.

Glory be to the Father and to the Son and to the Holy Ghost. As it was in the beginning, is now, and ever shall be, world without end. Amen.

13

Arise, O Lord, and let Thine enemies be scattered, and let them that hate Thee flee from before Thy Face. (X3)

14

On the Holy Face Medal pray: God, our Protector, look on us, and cast Thy eyes upon the Face of Thy Christ. Amen.

On the Crucifix make the sign of the Cross.

ADDITIONAL PRAYERS

ETERNAL FATHER, I offer Thee the Cross of our Lord Jesus Christ and all the other instruments of His Holy Passion, that Thou mayst put division in the camp of Thine enemies, as Thy beloved Son has said: "A kingdom divided against itself shall fall".

May the thrice Holy Name of God overthrow all their plans.

May the Name of the Living God split them up by disagreements.

May the terrible Name of the God of Eternity stamp out all their godlessness!

O Lord, I desire not the death of the sinner, but that he be converted and live: "Father, forgive them for they know not what they do."

Nihil Obstat: Fr. Thomas Hoisington, S.T.L. Censor Librorum April 11, 2025

Imprimatur: ✠ Bishop Carl A. Kemme Bishop of Wichita April 11, 2025

The Little Chaplet of the Holy Face

The little chaplet of the Holy Face is to be prayed using a special chaplet of beads that consists of thirty-three beads made up of five sets of six beads, and one set containing three beads. The first five sets are prayed to make reparation for the many sins and offences against Our Blessed Lord's Holy Face experienced through His five senses: touch, hearing, sight, smell, and taste. The remaining set of three beads is prayed in honour of the three years of our Blessed Lord's public ministry on earth.

A diagram is included in this chapter for instructional purposes.

1. On the Crucifix, make the Sign of the Cross and *pray*:

   O God, come to my assistance; O Lord, make haste to help me. Glory be to the Father, and to the Son, and to the Holy Ghost. As it was in the beginning, is now, and ever shall be, world without end. Amen.

2. *Pray:* My Jesus Mercy. **In Honour of the Sense of Touch**. Glory be to the Father, and to the Son, and to the Holy Ghost. As it was in the beginning, is now, and ever shall be, world without end. Amen.

3. *Invocation:*

Arise, O Lord, and let Thine enemies be scattered, and let them that hate Thee flee from before Thy Face. (×6)

4. *Pray:* My Jesus Mercy. **In Honour of the Sense of Hearing**. Glory be to the Father, and to the Son, and to the Holy Ghost. As it was in the beginning, is now, and ever shall be, world without end. Amen.

5. *Invocation:*

Arise, O Lord, and let Thine enemies be scattered, and let them that hate Thee flee from before Thy Face. (×6)

6. *Pray:* My Jesus Mercy. **In Honour of the Sense of Sight**. Glory be to the Father, and to the Son, and to the Holy Ghost. As it was in the beginning, is now, and ever shall be, world without end. Amen.

7. *Invocation:*

Arise, O Lord, and let Thine enemies be scattered, and let them that hate Thee flee from before Thy Face. (×6)

8. *Pray:* My Jesus Mercy. **In Honour of the Sense of Smell.** Glory be to the Father, and to the Son, and to the Holy Ghost. As it was in the beginning, is now, and ever shall be, world without end. Amen.

9. *Invocation:*

Arise, O Lord, and let Thine enemies be scattered, and let them that hate Thee flee from before Thy Face. (×6)

10. *Pray:* My Jesus Mercy. **In Honour of the Sense of Taste.** Glory be to the Father, and to the Son, and to the Holy Ghost. As it was in the beginning, is now, and ever shall be, world without end. Amen.

11. *Invocation:*

Arise, O Lord, and let Thine enemies be scattered, and let them that hate Thee flee from before Thy Face. (×6)

12. *Pray:* My Jesus Mercy. **Let Us Recall the Public Life of the Saviour and let us honour all the wounds of His adorable Face.** Glory be to the Father, and to the Son, and to the Holy Ghost. As it was in the beginning, is now, and ever shall be, world without end. Amen.

13. *Invocation:*

Arise, O Lord, and let Thine enemies be scattered, and let them that hate Thee flee from before Thy Face. (×3)

14. On the Holy Face Medal, pray:

God, our Protector, look on us, and cast Thy eyes upon the Face of Thy Christ. Amen.

Most beautiful Face of Jesus, so full of pity and sweetness, turn towards us Thy merciful gaze, and have compassion on us. May we never turn our eyes away from Thee but seek Thee in all creatures. May Thy image be ever imprinted in our hearts. Amen.

Consecration to the Holy Face

I ...., in order to give still greater increase to the glory of Jesus, dying for our salvation upon the Cross; in order to correspond to the merciful love with which His Holy Face is animated towards poor sinners, and in order to repair the outrages which the frightful crimes of the present day inflict upon His august Face, the most pure mirror of the divine Majesty, I associate myself, fully and freely, to the faithful received into this pious confraternity; I desire to participate in the indulgences with which it is enriched and in the good works practiced therein, as well for the expiation of my sins as for the solace of souls suffering in Purgatory.

Amiable Redeemer, most sweet Jesus, hide in the secret of Thy Face all the members of this association; may they there find shelter from the seductions of the world, and the snares of Satan; grant that, faithfully keeping all the precepts of Thy law and fulfilling the special duties of their state, they may be more and more inflamed with zeal for reparation, and with the flames of Thy divine love.

Weapons of the Passion

"The weapons of my enemies give death, but Mine give life."

I have already told you that I hold you in My hands as an arrow. I now want to hurl this arrow against my enemies. To arm you for the battle ahead, I give you the weapons of My Passion, that is My Cross, which these enemies dread, and also the other instruments of My tortures.

Go forward to meet those foes with the artlessness of a child and the bravery of a courageous soldier. Receive this mission in the benediction of the Father, of the Son, and of the Holy Ghost.

— Words of Our Lord to Sr. Marie de Saint-Pierre, March 29, 1847

Daily Prayers for Archconfraternity Members

(In Reparation for Sins Against the First Three Commandments)

Our Father

Our Father, who art in heaven,
hallowed be thy name.
Thy kingdom come, thy will be done,
on earth, as it is in heaven.
Give us this day our daily bread
and forgive us our trespasses
as we forgive those who trespass against us,
and lead us not into temptation,
but deliver us from evil. Amen.

Pater Noster (In Latin)

Pater noster, qui es in cælis,
sanctificétur nomen tuum.
Advéniat regnum tuum. Fiat voluntas tua,
sicut in cælo, et in terra.
Panem nostrum cotidiánum da nobis hódie,
et dimítte nobis débita nostra
sicut et nos dimíttimus debitóribus nostris.
Et ne nos indúcas in tentatiónem,
sed líbera nos a malo. Amen.

Hail Mary

Hail Mary, Full of Grace,
The Lord is with thee.
Blessed art thou among women,
and blessed is the fruit of thy womb, Jesus.
Holy Mary, Mother of God,
pray for us sinners now,
and at the hour of our death. Amen.

Ave Maria (In Latin)

Ave María, grátia plena,
Dóminus tecum.
Benedícta tu in muliéribus,
et benedíctus fructus ventris tui, Jesus.
Sancta María, Mater Dei,
ora pro nobis peccatóribus,
nunc, et in hora mortis nostræ. Amen.

Glory Be

Glory be to the Father,
and to the Son,
and to the Holy Spirit.
As it was in the beginning,
is now, and ever shall be,
world without end. Amen.

Gloria Patri (In Latin)

Glória Patri,
et Fílio,
et Spirítui Sancto.
Sicut erat in princípio,
et nunc, et semper,
et in sǽcula sæculórum. Amen.

Lord Show Us Thy Face

Show Us Thy Face
O' Lord, show us Thy Face
and we shall be saved.

(In Latin)

Ostende Nobis Faciem Tuam
(Dómine, osténde Fáciem tuam
et sálvi érimus.)

The Golden Arrow Prayer

May the most holy, most sacred, most adorable, most incomprehensible, and ineffable Name of God be for ever praised, blessed, loved, adored, and glorified, in heaven, on earth, and in hell, by all the creatures of God, and by the Sacred Heart of Our Lord Jesus Christ in the most Holy Sacrament of the Altar. Amen.

Five Additional Prayers from Jesus

1. Eternal Father, I offer Thee the Cross of our Lord Jesus Christ and all the other instruments of His Holy Passion, that Thou mayst put division in the camp of Thine enemies, as Thy beloved Son has said: "A kingdom divided against itself shall fall."

2. May the thrice Holy Name of God overthrow all their plans.

3. May the Holy Name of the Living God split them up by disagreements!

4. May the terrible Name of the God of Eternity stamp out all their godlessness.

5. O Lord, I desire not the death of the sinner, but that he be converted and live: "Father, forgive them for they know not what they do."

Appendix II:
Prayers of the Holy Face Devotion
(Rosary of the Holy Face)

JOYFUL MYSTERIES

1st Joyful Mystery: The Annunciation

I adore Thee, O Jesus, who, having the divine nature, didst deign to take upon Thyself our likeness in order to conform us all to Thy semblance.

Imprint more and more deeply in our souls, by a lively faith, the seal of Thy divine resemblance. Pardon, mercy for all unhappy pagans who are enemies of the Gospel, and rebel to the grace of Thy Incarnation.

2nd Joyful Mystery: The Visitation

I adore Thee, O Jesus, divine sun, whose rays, though veiled, reach him, « who is one day to walk before Thy Face. »

May the light of Thy Face, which descended upon us at the moment of baptism, enlighten, warm, and continually vivify our souls.

Pardon, mercy for all ungrateful men who desire to efface from their foreheads the mark of a Christian; for heretics who are not blessed by Thy luminous presence in the bosom of the true Church.

3rd Joyful Mystery: The Nativity

I adore Thee, O Jesus, little Infant laid in a crib. Thy Face, so full of graces, inspires angelic songs and ravishes the shepherds and the Magi.

All thy features wear an expression of benignity: *Apparuit benignitas* (Kindness appeared).

O beauty of the Holy Face, O goodness of Jesus, captivate all hearts!

Pardon, mercy for the many indifferent men who misunderstand Thy sweet attractions, who shut their hearts to the excess of Thy charity.

4th Joyful Mystery: The Purification

I adore Thee, O Jesus, presented in the Temple by the hands of Mary. Thou art the victim without spot, alone worthy of all the complaisance of the Father.

May we, like the holy old man Simeon, after having known and contemplated Thee with the eyes of faith, no longer cling to this world, but turn our eyes and our hearts to Thee alone.

Pardon, mercy for so many poor madmen, who are captivated and seduced by the figure of this world which passes away.

5th Joyful Mystery: The Finding of Jesus in the Temple

I adore Thee, O Jesus, found again in the temple in the midst of the Doctors. How beautiful was the ray of divine light, emanating from Thy august Face upon those who listened to Thee!

Make that wisdom, which Thou earnest to bring down upon earth, and which Thou hast placed within the reach of all, shine upon us.

Pardon, mercy for the voluntarily blind who obstinately refuse Thy light, and for the victims of an education without God.

SORROWFUL MYSTERIES

1st Sorrowful Mystery: The Agony in the Garden

Hail, adorable Face of my Saviour, bowed to the earth under the weight of the sins of the world which cover Thee with confusion. Take away from us all human respect, all culpable shame.

Eternal Father, I offer Thee the Face of Thy Son, covered with the sweat of agony, obscured by the shades of death; may Thy justice be appeased at the sight of so affecting a spectacle; mayest Thou have mercy on our country in spite of all the crimes that are committed against Thee therein.

2nd Sorrowful Mystery: The Scourging at the Pillar

Hail, adorable Face of my Saviour, disfigured by the scourges of the executioners, filled with fury against their innocent victim. Repair the injuries inflicted upon my soul by sin, which, as a hideous leprosy, disfigures and withers it.

Eternal Father, I offer Thee the bleeding Face of Thy Son in reparation for the innumerable, abominable sins, which imprint their shameful marks even upon the face of men.

3rd Sorrowful Mystery: The Crowning with Thorns

Hail, adorable Face of my Saviour, ignominiously blindfolded, covered with spittle, crowned with thorns, wounded with blows. Efface from amongst us every trace of that devastating scourge, the impious and satanic pride of our epoch.

Eternal Father, I offer Thee the Face of Thy Son, which has become unrecognizable. Spare us, and our nation, which has committed so many blasphemies, so many profanations, so many audacious revolts against Thee.

4th Sorrowful Mystery: The Bearing of the Cross

Hail, adorable Face of my Saviour, miraculously impressed upon the veil of St. Veronica. May my soul bear the impress of the features of Thy humiliation, so that it may be one day clothed with Thy glory!

Eternal Father, I offer Thee the Face of Thy Son still wiped by so many faithful Veronicas, by so many reparatory souls. For the sake of these souls which are so pleasing to Thee, stay Thy chastisements, and do not hurl Thy avenging thunders upon our unhappy people.

5th Sorrowful Mystery: The Crucifixion

Hail, adorable Face of my Saviour on the Cross. Before Thee, the sun is veiled, the earth is moved and is covered with darkness, all nature mourns.

O features of the dying Jesus, features of crucified love, the ineffable expression of which has ravished all the saints! May you be imprinted deeply in my heart!

Eternal Father, I offer Thee the Face of Thy expiring Son.

Respice in Faciem Christi tui! « Look on the Face of Thy Christ. »

May Thy bowels be moved and may the flood of Thy mercy inundate the whole earth.

GLORIOUS MYSTERIES

1st Glorious Mystery: The Resurrection

Glory to Thee, O Lord, risen Jesus, who didst appear with radiant Face to Thy mother, to the holy women, to the assembled disciples.

It is no longer Calvary with its horrors. What beauty, what splendour, what gladness! By that glory of Thy Face, give back to our souls the beauty of which sin has deprived them; give back to them their Christian characteristics.

2nd Glorious Mystery: The Ascension

Glory to Thee, Lord Jesus, ascending to heaven, with Thy Face turned towards the shores of Thy blessed home. Thou wilt hereafter descend once more with the angry Face of the judge, and in the presence of Thy Majesty, every proud head shall prostrate itself before Thee. O sweet Face of Jesus, going to prepare a place for us, charm our eyes, raise our gaze towards Thee! We desire to belong « to the generation of those who, thirsting, seek the Face of the God of Jacob ».

3rd Glorious Mystery: The Descent of the Holy Ghost

Glory to Thee, Lord Jesus, seated at the right hand of the Father. Thou wilt appear continually before the Face of God to plead our cause. A thousand and a thousand thanksgivings for that perpetual intercession. After having obtained the full effusion of the Holy Spirit upon the apostles, pray to Thy Father to let the same Holy Spirit reign over us, let it brood upon the face of the great waters, upon the nations of the earth agitated, like an ocean, by the tempests of atheism.

4th Glorious Mystery: The Assumption

Glory to Thee, Lord Jesus, the new Solomon coming to meet Thy mother. How beautiful Thou art, how gracious, how full of infinite amiability in the presence of the holy ark introduced by Thee into the heavenly Jerusalem amidst celestial songs!

O smiling Face of Jesus, appear to us at the hour of death, and may the horrible form of the devil disappear at Thy aspect.

5th Glorious Mystery: The Crowning of the Virgin

Glory to Thee, Lord Jesus, crowning Thy mother, and making her sit down beside Thee. The eyes of all the Blessed are fixed on Thy Face and on that of Thy mother. Those two Faces shine like two suns and shed joy throughout the whole of Paradise. O Jesus, O Mary, grant us the grace so greatly to be desired, the grace of graces, that of contemplating you hereafter face to face in the eternal vision of the elect.

Litany of the Holy Face

(Composed by Sr. Marie de Saint-Pierre)

In Reparation for Blasphemies, and to Implore of God, by the Adorable Face of His Son, the conversion of Blasphemers.

Let us pray:

Lord, have mercy on us. Christ, have mercy on us.

Lord, have mercy on us. Christ, hear us.

Christ, graciously hear us. Holy Virgin Mary, pray for us.

O Jesus, whose adorable Face was adored with profound respect by Mary and Joseph when they saw You for the first time, have mercy on us.

O Jesus, whose adorable Face ravished with joy the angels, shepherds, and Magi in the stable of Bethlehem, have mercy on us.

O Jesus, whose adorable Face was wounded with a dart of love, the aged Simeon and the prophetess Anna in the temple, have mercy on us.

O Jesus, whose adorable Face was bathed in tears in Your holy Infancy, have mercy on us.

O Jesus, whose adorable Face was filled with admiration, the doctors in the temple, have mercy on us.

O Jesus, the charms and grace of whose adorable Face win all hearts, have mercy on us.

O Jesus, whose adorable Face is characterized by nobility, have mercy on us.

O Jesus, whose adorable Face is the admiration of the angels, have mercy on us.

O Jesus, whose adorable Face is the sweet delight of the Saints, have mercy on us.

O Jesus, whose adorable Face is the masterpiece of the Holy Spirit, in which the Eternal Father is well pleased, have mercy on us.

O Jesus, whose adorable Face is the delight of Mary and Joseph, have mercy on us.

O Jesus, whose adorable Face is the ineffable mirror of the Divine Perfections, have mercy on us.

O Jesus, the beauty of whose adorable Face is ever ancient and ever new, have mercy on us.

O Jesus, whose adorable Face, full of modesty and sweetness, attracted the just and the sinners, have mercy on us.

O Jesus, whose adorable Face appeases the anger of God, have mercy on us.

O Jesus, whose adorable Face is the terror of the evil spirits, have mercy on us.

O Jesus, whose adorable Face is the treasure of graces and blessings, have mercy on us.

O Jesus, whose adorable Face was exposed to the inclemency of the weather in the desert, have mercy on us.

O Jesus, whose adorable Face was scorched by the sun and bathed in sweat on Your journeys, have mercy on us.

O Jesus, the expression of whose adorable Face is wholly Divine, have mercy on us.

O Jesus, whose adorable Face sorrowed and wept at the tomb of Lazarus, have mercy on us.

O Jesus, whose adorable Face was brilliant as the sun and radiant with glory on Mount Tabor, have mercy on us.

O Jesus, whose adorable Face is worthy of all reverence, veneration, and worship, have mercy on us.

O Jesus, whose adorable Face grew sad at the sight of Jerusalem when You did weep over that ungrateful city, have mercy on us.

O Jesus, whose adorable Face was bowed down to the ground in the garden of Olives, and covered with confusion for our sins, have mercy on us.

O Jesus, whose adorable Face was bathed in a bloody sweat, have mercy on us.

O Jesus, whose adorable Face was kissed by the traitor Judas, have mercy on us.

O Jesus, the sanctity and majesty of whose adorable Face smote the soldiers with fear and cast them down, have mercy on us.

O Jesus, whose adorable Face was struck by a vile servant, shamefully blindfolded and profaned by the sacrilegious hands of Your enemies, have mercy on us.

O Jesus, whose adorable Face was defiled with spittle, and bruised with so many buffets and blows, Have mercy on us.

O Jesus, the divine look of whose adorable Face wounded the heart of Peter with repentant love, have mercy on us.

O Jesus, whose adorable Face was humbled for us at the tribunals of Jerusalem, have mercy on us.

O Jesus, whose adorable Face did preserve Your serenity when Pilate pronounced the fatal sentence, Have mercy on us.

O Jesus, the brow of whose adorable Face was crowned with thorns, have mercy on us.

O Jesus, whose adorable Face covered with sweat and Blood fell in the mire under the heavy weight of the Cross, have mercy on us.

O Jesus, whose adorable Face was wiped by the pious Veronica on the way to Calvary, Have mercy on us.

O Jesus, whose adorable Face was raised on the instrument of the most shameful punishment, have mercy on us.

O Jesus, the eyes of whose adorable Face were filled with tears of Blood, have mercy on us.

O Jesus, the mouth of whose adorable Face was filled with vinegar and gall, have mercy on us.

O Jesus, the incomparable beauty of whose adorable Face was obscured under the dreadful cloud of the sins of the world, have mercy on us.

O Jesus, whose adorable Face was covered with the sad shades of death, have mercy on us.

O Jesus, whose adorable Face was washed and anointed by Mary and the holy women and wrapped in a shroud, have mercy on us.

O Jesus, whose adorable Face was enclosed in the sepulchre, Have mercy on us.

O Jesus, whose adorable Face was all resplendent with glory and beauty on the day of Your Resurrection, have mercy on us.

O Jesus, whose adorable Face was dazzling with light at the moment of Your Ascension, have mercy on us.

O Jesus, whose adorable Face is hidden in the Eucharist, Have mercy on us.

O Jesus, whose adorable Face will appear at the end of time in the clouds with great power and majesty, have mercy on us.

O Jesus, whose adorable Face will cause the wicked to tremble, Have mercy on us.

O Jesus, whose adorable Face will fill the just with joy for all eternity, Have mercy on us.

Lamb of God, who takes away the sins of the world, Spare us, O Lord.

Lamb of God, who takes away the sins of the world, graciously hear us, O Lord.

Lamb of God, who takes away the sins of the world, have mercy on us.

By a Rescript dated 27th of January 1853, His Holiness Pope Pius IX grants to all who recite, with a contrite heart, these prayers in honour of the Holy Face of Jesus Christ an indulgence of a hundred days for each line; applicable to the souls in Purgatory.

Litany of the Holy Face (Shorter Version)

I salute Thee, I adore Thee, and I love Thee, O adorable Face of Jesus, my Beloved, noble Seal of the Divinity! Outraged anew by blasphemers. I offer Thee, through the heart of Thy blessed Mother, the worship of all the Angels and Saints, most humbly beseeching Thee to repair and renew in me and in all men Thine Image disfigured by sin.

Let us pray:

O adorable Face, which was adored, with profound respect, by Mary and Joseph when they saw Thee, for the first time, have mercy on us,

O adorable Face, which ravished with joy, in the stable of Bethlehem, the Angels, the shepherds, and the magi, have mercy on us,

O adorable Face, which transpierced with a dart of love in the Temple, the saintly old man Simeon and the prophetess Anna, have mercy on us,

O adorable Face, which filled with admiration the Doctors of the Law when Thou appeared in the Temple at the age of twelve years, have mercy on us,

O adorable Face, which possesses beauty always ancient and always new, have mercy on us,

O adorable Face, which is the masterpiece of the Holy Ghost, in which the Eternal Father is well pleased, have mercy on us,

O adorable Face, which is the ineffable mirror of the divine perfections, have mercy on us,

O adorable Face of Jesus, which was so mercifully bowed down on the Cross, on the day of Thy Passion, for the salvation of the world! Once more today, in pity, bend down towards us poor sinners. Cast upon us a glance of compassion and give us Thy peace.

O adorable Face which became brilliant like the sun and radiant with glory, on the Mountain of Tabor, have mercy on us,

O adorable Face which wept and was troubled at the tomb of Lazarus, have mercy on us,

O adorable Face, which was rendered sad at the sight of Jerusalem, and shed tears on that ungrateful city, have mercy on us,

O adorable Face, which was bowed down to the ground in the Garden of Olives, and covered with confusion for our sins, have mercy on us,

O adorable Face, which was covered with the sweat of blood, have mercy on us,

O adorable Face, which was struck by a vile servant, covered with a veil of shame, and profaned by the sacrilegious hands of Thine enemies, have mercy on us,

O adorable Face which, by its divine glance, wounded the heart of St. Peter with a dart of sorrow and love, have mercy on us,

Be merciful to us, O my God!

Do not reject our prayers when in the midst of our afflictions, we call upon Thy Holy Name and seek with love and confidence Thine adorable Face.

O adorable Face, which was washed and anointed by Mary and the holy women and covered with a shroud, have mercy on us,

O adorable Face, which was all resplendent with glory and beauty on the day of the Resurrection, have mercy on us,

O adorable Face which is hidden in the Eucharist, have mercy on us,

O adorable Face which will appear at thc end of time in the clouds with great power and great majesty, have mercy on us,

O adorable Face which will make sinners tremble, have mercy on us,

O adorable Face which will fill the just with joy for all eternity, have mercy on us,

O adorable Face which merits all our reverence, our homage and our adoration, have mercy on us,

O Lord, show us Thy Face, and we shall be saved!

O Lord, show us Thy Face, and we shall be saved!

O Lord, show us Thy Face, and we shall be saved!

Litany to Obtain Humility

Lord, have pity on me.

O Jesus, meek and humble of Heart, hear me.

O Jesus, Meek and humble of Heart, graciously hear me.

From the desire of being esteemed, Deliver me, Jesus.

From the desire of being loved, Deliver me, Jesus.

From the desire of being sought after, Deliver me, Jesus.

From the desire of being praised, Deliver me, Jesus.

From the desire of being honoured, Deliver me, Jesus.

From the desire of being preferred, Deliver me, Jesus.

From the desire of being consulted, Deliver me, Jesus.

From the desire of being approved, Deliver me, Jesus.

From the desire of being humoured, Deliver me, Jesus.

From the fear of being humbled, Deliver me, Jesus.

From the fear of being despised, Deliver me, Jesus.

From the fear of suffering rebuffed, Deliver me, Jesus.

From the fear of being calumniated, Deliver me, Jesus.

From the fear of being forgotten, Deliver me, Jesus.

From the fear of being mocked at, Deliver me, Jesus.

From the desire of being scoffed, Deliver me, Jesus.

From the fear of being insulted, Deliver me, Jesus.

O Mary, mother of the humble, pray for me.

Saint Joseph, protector of humble souls, pray for me.

Saint Michael, who was the first to tread pride under foot, pray for me.

All the just who are sanctified, above all, by the spirit of humility, pray for me.

Invocation

O Jesus, whose first lesson was this: "*Learn of me, who am meek and humble of heart*", teach me to become humble of heart like Thee. Amen.

Exercise in Honour of Our Lady
of the Seven Dolours

First Sorrow of Mary – The Prophecy of St. Simeon

I deeply compassionate, O Mary, mother of sorrows, the affliction suffered by thy tender heart, on hearing the prophecy of the old man Simeon. Dearest mother, by thy greatly afflicted heart, obtain for us the virtue of humility and the grace of the fear of God.

Pray: Hail Mary / Ave Maria

Second Sorrow of Mary – The Flight into Egypt

I deeply compassionate, O Mary, mother of sorrows, the anguish suffered by thy most sensitive heart during the flight and the sojourn in Egypt. Dearest mother, by thy afflicted heart, obtain for us the virtue of generosity and of liberality above all towards the poor and the gift of piety.

Pray: Hail Mary / Ave Maria

Third Sorrow of Mary – The Loss of the Child Jesus in the Temple

I deeply compassionate, O Mary, mother of sorrows, the cruel grief felt by thy tender heart, at the loss of thy dear Son Jesus. Dearest mother, by thy holy heart so keenly tried, obtain for us the virtue of chastity and the gift of knowledge.

Pray: Hail Mary / Ave Maria

Fourth Sorrow of Mary – Meeting Jesus on the Way of the Cross

I deeply compassionate, O Mary, mother of sorrows, the consternation which thy maternal heart experienced when thou didst meet Jesus bearing His Cross. Dearest mother, by Thy sensitive heart so steeped in bitterness, obtain for us the virtue of patience and the gift of fortitude.

Pray: Hail Mary / Ave Maria

Fifth Sorrow of Mary – The Crucifixion of Jesus

I deeply compassionate, O Mary, mother of sorrows, the martyrdom endured by thy courageous heart at witnessing Jesus in his agony. Dearest mother, by thy heart, so cruelly martyred, obtain for us the virtue of temperance and the gift of good counsel.

Pray: Hail Mary / Ave Maria

Sixth Sorrow of Mary – The Taking of the Body of Jesus Down from the Cross

I deeply compassionate, O Mary, mother of sorrows, the wound received by thy tender heart when the side of Jesus was opened, and his Heart pierced by the lance. Dearest mother, by thy heart so sorrowfully transpierced, obtain for us the virtue of fraternal charity and the gift of understanding.

Pray: Hail Mary / Ave Maria

Seventh Sorrow of Mary – The Laying of the Body of Jesus in the Tomb

I deeply compassionate, O Mary, mother of sorrows, the lively anguish with which Thy tender heart was torn at the burial of Jesus. Dearest mother, by thy sacred heart, so cruelly overwhelmed by sorrow, obtain for us the virtue of diligence and the gift of wisdom.

Pray: Hail Mary / Ave Maria

V) Pray for us, O most sorrowful Virgin.

R) That we may be made worthy of the promises of Christ.

Prayer:

Lord Jesus, we implore, now and for the hour of our death, the intercession of the most blessed Virgin Mary, Thy mother, whose holy soul was transpierced, at the time of Thy Passion, with a sword of grief. Grant this, O Saviour of the world, Thou who livest and reignest with the Father and the Holy Ghost for ever and ever. Amen.

The Seven Aves, In Honour of Mary, Mother of Dolours

Anyone who will recite, with a contrite heart, seven Aves, Maria, adding, after each one of them, this invocation: **Holy mother, engrave the wounds of my Saviour in my innermost heart**, will gain: firstly an indulgence of 300 days, once a day; and secondly a plenary indulgence, once a month, if recited every day.

Appendix III:
Treasury of Prayers and Reflections

The Nine Promises of the Holy Face Devotion

1. They shall receive in themselves, by the impression of My Humanity, a bright irradiation from My Divinity, and shall be so illuminated by it in their inmost souls that by their likeness to My Face they shall shine with the brightness surpassing that of many others in eternal life. (St. Gertrude, *Insinuations*, book IV, ch. VII)

2. St. Mechtilde, having asked our Lord that those who celebrate the memory of His sweet Face should never be deprived of His amiable company, He replied: "Not one of them shall be separated from Me." (St. Mechtilde, *Of Spiritual Grace*, book I, ch. XIII)

3. "Our Lord," said Sister Marie de Saint-Pierre, "has promised me that He will imprint His Divine likeness on the souls of those who honor His most Holy Countenance." (January 21, 1847) "This adorable Face is, as it were, the seal of the Divinity, which has the virtue of reproducing the likeness of

God in the souls that are appied to it." (Novemeber 6, 1845)

4. "By My Holy Face you shall work miracles." (Our Lord to Sister Marie de Saint-Pierre, October 27, 1845)

5. "By My Holy Face, you will obtain the conversion of many sinners. Nothing that you ask in making this offering will be refused to you. No one can know how pleasing the sight of My Face is to My Father!" (Our Lord to Sister Marie de Saint-Pierre, November 22, 1846)

6. As in a kingdom, you can procure all you wish with a coin stamped with the prince's effigy, so in the Kingdom of Heaven, you will obtain all you desire with the precious coin of My Holy Humanity, which is My adorable Countenance." (Our Lord to Sister Marie de Saint-Pierre, October 29, 1845)

7. "All those who honor My Holy Face in a spirit of reparation will be so doing perform the office of the pious Veronica." (Our Lord to Sister Marie de Saint-Pierre, October 27, 1845).

8. "According to the care you take in making reparation to My Face, disfigured by blasphemies, so will I take care of your soul, which has been disfigured by sin. I will reprint My image and render it as beautiful as it was on leaving the baptismal font." (Our Lord to Sister Marie de Saint-Pierre, November 3, 1845)

9. "Our Lord promised me, said again Sister Saint-Pierre, for all those who defend His cause in this Work of Reparation, by words, by prayers, or in writing, that He will defend them before His Father; at their death, He will purify their souls by effacing all the blots of sin and will restore to them their primitive beauty." (March 12, 1846)

Prayers and Meditations from St. Thérèse of the Child Jesus and of the Holy Face

These prayers from St. Thérèse of Lisieux, the famous Carmelite nun known affectionately as the "Little Flower", reflect her great love and devotion to our Lord Jesus Christ in His Holy Face. St. Thérèse entered the Carmelite convent in Lisieux, France, when she was only 15, in 1888, and died there from tuberculosis in 1897.

Her autobiography, *Story of a Soul*, published after her death, inspired people all over the world with its moving message of love for Jesus. That book, along with the various miracles attributed to her after her death, led to her canonization by Pope Pius XI in 1925. This prayer below reflects St. Thérèse's special sanctity, as well as her deep humility. It is no wonder that she took the name as a religious of "Sister Thérèse of the Child Jesus and the Holy Face"!

Prayer

"O Jesus, who, in Thy cruel Passion didst become the 'reproach of men and the Man of Sorrows,' I worship Thy divine Face. Once it shone with the beauty and sweetness of the Divinity, but now, for my sake, it has become as 'the face of a leper.' Yet, in that disfigured Countenance, I recognize Thy infinite love, and I am consumed with the desire of making Thee loved by all mankind. The tears that flowed so abundantly from Thy Eyes are to me as precious pearls that I delight to gather, that with their worth I may ransom the souls of poor sinners. O Jesus, whose Face is the sole beauty that ravishes my heart, I may not see here below the sweetness of Thy glance, nor feel the ineffable tenderness of Thy kiss, I bow to Thy Will — but I pray Thee to imprint in me Thy divine likeness, and I implore Thee so to inflame me with Thy love, that it may quickly consume me, and that I may soon reach the vision of Thy glorious Face in heaven. Amen."

St. Thérèse is best known for her approach to spirituality, known as the "Little Way", which has inspired holiness in countless numbers of the faithful. She realized that she wasn't meant to do great heroic deeds like, for example, St. Joan of Arc, in service to our Lord. Her calling was rather to serve Him with great love in her daily errands and sacrifices, offering up to God her sufferings and her smallness.

St. Thérèse was inspired in part by this line from scripture: "Whoever is a little one, let him come to me" (Proverbs 9:4). She once wrote, "I rejoice in my littleness, because only little children and those who are like them shall be admitted to the Heavenly Banquet."

She also felt closer to Jesus, particularly in His Passion, in contemplation of His Holy Face, which strengthened her desire, born out of a loving humility, to do our Lord's work "hidden" and "forgotten," as she put it. This recalls the great line in Scripture from John the Baptist when He said of Jesus, "He must increase, but I must decrease" (John 3:30).

Holy Face Prayer for Sinners

Eternal Father, since Thou hast given me for my inheritance the Adorable Face of Thy Divine Son, I offer that face to Thee and I beg Thee, in exchange for this coin of infinite value, to forget the ingratitude of souls dedicated to Thee and to pardon all poor sinners.

Jesus, Your ineffable image is the star which guides my steps. Ah, You know, Your sweet Face is for me, Heaven on earth. My love discovers the charms of Your Face adorned with tears. I smile through my own tears when I contemplate Your sorrows.

St. Thérèse also wrote this moving Canticle to the Holy Face, which highlights her devotion to Jesus in His Holy Face quite well, as we read in this translation below from the original French:

Jesus! Thy dear and holy Face
Is the bright star that guides my way;
Thy gentle glance, so full of grace,
Is my true heaven on earth, today.
My love finds out the holy charm
Of Thy dear eyes with tear-drops wet;
Through mine own tears I smile at Thee,
And in Thy griefs my pains forget.
Oh! I would gladly live unknown,
Thus to console Thy aching heart.
Thy veiled beauty, it is shown
To those who live from earth apart.
Fain would I fly to Thee alone!
Thy Face, it is my fatherland;
It is the sunshine of my days;
My realm of love, my sunlit land,
Where, through the hours, I sing Thy praise;
It is the lily of the vale,

Whose mystic perfume, freely given,

Brings comfort when I faint and fail,

And makes me taste the peace of heaven.

Thy face, in its unearthly grace,

Is like the divinest myrrh to me,

That on my heart I gladly place;

It is my lyre of melody;

My rest - my comfort - is Thy Face.

My only wealth, Lord! is thy Face;

Naught ask I more than this from Thee;

Hidden in the secret of Thy Face,

The more I shall resemble Thee!

Leave on me the divine impress

Of Thy sweet, patient Face of love,

And soon I shall become a saint,

And draw men's hearts to Thee above.

So, in the secret of Thy Face,

Oh! Hide me, hide me, Jesus blest!

There let me find its hidden grace,

Its holy fires, and, in heaven's rest,

Its rapturous kiss, in Thy embrace!

St. Thérèse read the book on the life of Sr. Marie de Saint Pierre, given to her by her older sister (Pauline), and she carried a locket of hair and kept a small picture of Sr. Marie de Saint Pierre. She composed canticles and prayers to the Holy Face.

"Oh, I would wish to tell everybody to study and venerate an Image of the Holy Face as He left it on Veronica's Veil. When sorrow strikes, it will be the only consolation. No matter what our grief, surely it will never be as fearful as was His!"

"Look at His adorable Face, His glazed and sunken eyes, His wounds. Look Jesus in the Face. There you will see how He loves us." St. Thérèse of Lisieux

"Your Veiled Gaze is Our Heaven…"St. Thérèse of Lisieux

St. Thérèse's sister Celine (Sr. Genevieve of the Holy Face) also wrote: "Devotion to the Holy Face was, for St. Thérèse, the crown and complement of her love for the Sacred Humanity of Our Lord. The Blessed Face was the mirror wherein she beheld the Heart and Soul of her Well-Beloved. Just as the picture of a loved one serves to bring the whole person before us, so in the Holy Face of Christ, St. Thérèse beheld the entire Humanity of Jesus. We can say unequivocally that this devotion was the burning inspiration of the Saint's life... Her devotion to the Holy Face transcended, or more accurately, embraced, all the other attractions of her spiritual life."

St. Thérèse, her siblings, and her Father were all registered members with the Archconfraternity of the Holy Face in Tours, France.

St. Thérèse of the Child Jesus and of the Holy Face was born on January 2, 1873 and died on September 30, 1897.

Pious Reflections on The Holy Face taken from the Writings of Sister Marie de Saint Pierre

1. The Holy Face and the Holy Name of Jesus

A comparison as simple as it is just will enable us to see how the impious, by their blasphemies, attack the adorable Face of our Lord, and how faithful souls glorify it by the praises which they render to His Name and to His person.

Merit is in the persons, but the glory which accompanies them is in their name; it casts a lustre upon them when it is pronounced; the merit or demerit of a person is attached to his name.

The most holy Name of Jesus expresses the glorious victory which he has obtained over hell, and it embraces in it the infinite merits of His adorable person. The most holy Name of God expresses the Divinity, and it embraces in it all the perfections of the Creator. Hence, it follows that the blasphemers of these sacred Names attack God Himself.

Now, let us recall to mind those words of Jesus: *I am in my Father, and my Father is in me.* Jesus has rendered himself passable by the Incarnation; it is he who has suffered in his adorable Face the outrages inflicted upon the Name of God his Father by blasphemers.

There is something mysterious in the face of a man who is despised. Yes, I see that there is a particular link between his name and his face.

Look, He said, at a man distinguished by his name and through his merits in presence of his enemies; they do not indeed attack him with blows, but they overwhelm him with injuries; they affix derisive and bitter epithets to his name, instead of the titles which are his due. Then, observe what passes over the countenance of the man subjected to such insults; would you not say that all the outrageous words which issue from the mouth of his enemies fix themselves on his face, and cause him to suffer real torments? His brow is flushed and covered with shame and confusion; the opprobrium and ignominy he suffers are more cruel to bear than real torments in other parts of his body. Behold then herein a feeble portrait of the Face of our Lord, outraged by the blasphemies of the impious.

Let us now represent to ourselves the same man in presence of his friends, who, having heard of the insults he has received, hasten to console him, to treat him in accordance with his dignity, and to do homage to the greatness of his name, by giving him all the exalted titles to which he has a right. Then you see that the man's face reflects the pleasure these praises give him. Glory rests upon his brow, and, flowing down his face, renders it resplendent; joy shines in his eyes, there is a smile upon his lips; in a word, his faithful friends have healed the painful wounds inflicted on his face, outraged by his enemies; the glory has exceeded the opprobrium. Behold then, what the friends of Jesus perform by the work of reparation; the glory which they give to his Name rests upon His august brow and rejoices His most Holy Face in a very special manner in the most Holy Sacrament of the altar.

2. The Work of Reparation by Means of the Holy Face

This work has, for its main object, the reparation of blasphemies, and the reparation of the holy day of Sunday, profaned by secular labour; in consequence, it embraces the reparation of the outrages inflicted upon God and the sanctification of his Name.

Ought the devotion to the Holy Face to be united to this work? Yes, it is its riches and its most precious ornament, since our Lord has made a gift of His Holy Face to the work, in order to be the object of the devotion of the associates; they become all powerful with God through the offering which they ought to make to Him of this august and holy Face, the presence of which is so agreeable to Him that it infallibly appeases His anger and attracts His infinite mercy upon poor sinners. Yes, when the Eternal Father looks upon the Face of His well-beloved Son, which has been wounded by blows and covered with ignominy, the sight moves his bowels of compassion. Let us endeavour to profit by so precious a gift, and let us entreat the divine Saviour to hide us in the secret of His Face during the evil days.

3. Why the Holy Face is the Visible Sign of Reparation

The august Face offered to our adorations is the ineffable mirror of the divine perfections; perfections which are contained and expressed in the most holy Name of God.

As the Sacred Heart of Jesus is the visible sign offered to our adorations in order to represent his immense love in the most sacred Sacrament of the altar, so in like manner, the adorable Face of our Lord is the sensible object offered to our adorations, in order to repair the outrages committed by blasphemers against the Majesty and the Sovereignty of God, of which this Holy Face is the figure, the mirror and the expression; by the virtue of this Holy Face offered to the Eternal Father, His anger will be appeased and the conversion of the impious and of blasphemers obtained. It is true to say that blasphemers and sectarians inflict anew on the Holy Face of our Lord the ignominies of His Passion.

The impious who utter evil words and blaspheme the holy Name of God, spit in the Face of the Saviour and cover it with mud, whilst all the blows which sectarians give the Church and to religion, are the renewal of the numberless blows inflicted on the Face of our Lord, and which cause the divine Face to sweat afresh, because impious men strive to annihilate the fruit of his labours. Veronicas are required in order to wipe and to honour this august Face, which has so few worshippers. All those who apply themselves to this work of reparation, perform thereby the office of the pious Israelite.

4. Veronica and the Good Thief

The Saviour taught the Sister that two persons had rendered him a signal service during his Passion; the first was Veronica, who glorified His holy humanity by wiping His adorable Face on the path to Calvary; the second was the good thief, who, from the cross as from a pulpit, preached in defence of His cause and confessed His divinity whilst it was being blasphemed by the other thief and by the Jews.

« Our Lord made me to understand, » she says, « that two persons were to be our models and protectors, one of whom was Veronica, the model of persons of her sex who are not charged with defending His cause in public by their voices, but on whom it is incumbent to wipe His Holy Face by their prayers, praises and adorations. The other person was the good thief, the special model of men and of the ministers of the Church who are called, in the work of reparation, publicly to defend the honour of God, and to proclaim His glory in the face of those who outrage it. Therefore, as a recompense, the Saviour gave to Saint Veronica His adorable portrait and bestowed on the good thief an immediate entrance into His heavenly Kingdom.

Our Lord promised the Sister not to show Himself less magnificent towards those who, by their prayers, their adorations, or their writings, should boldly defend His cause before men, without being afraid of either their ill will or their powers.

5. Virtue of the Holy Face in Relation to St. Peter

There are men upon earth who possess the art of restoring bodies, but there is only our Lord who can be called the restorer of souls after the image of God. This then is the grace which the divine Master promises to grant to all who shall set themselves to render to His adorable Face the honour and the adoration which it merits, with the intention of repairing by this homage the opprobrium it receives from blasphemers.

We see in the apostle Saint Peter an example of the virtue of the Holy Face. The apostle had by his sin effaced the image of God in his soul, but Jesus turned his Holy Face towards the faithless apostle, and he became penitent. Jesus looked on Peter, and Peter wept bitterly.

The adorable Face is, as it were, the seal of the Divinity which has the power of re-impressing on souls to which it is applied the image of God.

6. The Holy Face Represents the Adorable Trinity

Remember, oh my soul, the sublime lesson which thy heavenly Spouse has given Thee in His adorable Face. Remember that this divine head represents the Eternal Father who is not engendered; the mouth of this Holy Face represents the Word engendered by the Father, and the two eyes of this mysterious Face represent the reciprocal love of the Father and of the Son; for these divine eyes have both of them but one and the same light, one and the same knowledge, and produce but one and the same love, represented by the Holy Spirit. Contemplate in the hair the infinity of the adorable perfections of the most Holy Trinity; see in that majestic Head the precious portion of the holy humanity of the Saviour, the image of the unity of God.

Prayers to the Holy Face Extracted from the Writings of Venerable Leo Dupont

I - Elevation of the Heart to Jesus, upon the outrages offered to His Holy Face.

Who can say how greatly our divine Saviour is offended by blasphemy! Placed as he is between his Father and sinners, the outrages which cannot rise as high as Heaven fall in a rain of ignominy upon his divine Face.

O Jesus! Thou must be God, since Thou art patient enough still to remain in our midst! If Thou couldst but find a sufficiency of friends possessed of the courage to interpose between Thee and the miserable people who conduct Thee back to Calvary!

But, as on the day of Thy Passion, Thou art alone amongst Thy enemies. Alas! Do we not run the risk of losing all if, illuminated by the light of faith which enables us to see what Thou art, O Jesus! Do we not at least imitate the witnesses of Thy death in their lively contrition? If it be not given to all of us to weep like Saint Peter, grant that we may strike our breasts like the populace which returned to Jerusalem, distracted with grief at recognizing the proof of a deicide.

O Holy Ghost! Thou who didst enlighten the Apostles and didst reanimate their courage so energetically, inflame us with Thy divine fire, put into our mouths burning words after having enkindled in our hearts the fire of Thy love, that becoming new men, we may feel ourselves possessed of sufficient courage to throw ourselves into the midst of the ranks of the enemy. Give us grace to vanquish them and to oblige them to love Thee. Amen.

II - Prayer of Reparation to the Holy Face

Lord Jesus! after having contemplated Thy features, disfigured by grief; after having meditated upon Thy Passion with compunction and love, how can our hearts help being inflamed with a holy hatred of sin, which even now, still outrages Thy adorable Face? But, not allowing ourselves to be content with mere compassion, give us grace to follow Thee so closely on this new Calvary, that the opprobrium destined for Thee may rebound upon us, O Jesus, and that we may at least have some small share in the expiation of sin. Amen.

III - Offering of the Holy Face
to the Eternal Father

Almighty God, Eternal Father, contemplate the Face of Thy Son, our Lord Jesus Christ. We present it to Thee with confidence for the glory of Thy Holy Name, for the exaltation of Thy holy Church, and for the salvation of the world. Most merciful Advocate, he opens his mouth to plead our cause; listen to his cries, behold his tears, O my God, and Thou wilt be touched with compassion towards the poor sinners who ask of Thee grace and mercy. Amen.

IV - Prayer to the Holy Face for
the Feast of the Dedication

O God ! who on the day of the dedication of the Temple, in an effusion of merciful goodness, didst promise to listen, from the height of heaven, to those who should invoke Thy Name, and who should seek Thy Face; grant to the associates of the Work of Reparation of blasphemy, prostrate before Thy adorable Face, the graces of which they have need in order efficaciously to work out their own salvation and to convert the blasphemers themselves, for whom Thy holy Name is invoked with confidence. Thou, who livest and reignest for ever and ever. Amen.

V - Aspiration Towards the Glorious Face of Our Lord

Lord! at the thought of the blessings which the vision of Thy Face could not but shed upon the earth, the Prophet exclaims in a holy transport:

"Happy the people who joyfully declare Thy glory…"

O Lord! permit us to aspire to this divine science, grant us to walk in the light of Thy Face, and to rejoice in the praises which we will offer by day and night to Thy holy Name.

(Ps. 88:15, 16, 17)

Some Short Prayers of Leo Dupont

O Saviour Jesus! At the sight of Thy most Holy Face, disfigured by grief, and at the sight of Thy Sacred Heart so full of love, I cry out with Saint Augustine: Lord Jesus, impress upon my heart Thy sacred wounds, that I may read therein at once Thy sorrow and Thy love; Thy sorrow, in order to suffer every affliction for Thee; Thy love, in order for Thee to despise every other love. Amen.

Lord Jesus! When presenting ourselves before Thy adorable Face to entreat Thee for the graces of which we have need, we beseech Thee, above all things, so to order the interior dispositions of our hearts, that we may never refuse Thee aught that Thou Thyself askest of us every day, through Thy holy commandments and by Thy divine inspirations. Amen.

O good Jesus, who hast said: "Ask, and you shall receive; seek, and you shall find; knock, and it shall be opened to you," give us, if it be Thy will, the faith which supplies all, or else supply Thyself all that is wanting in us of faith; grant us, by the sole effect of Thy charily and for Thy eternal glory, the graces of which we stand in need and which we look for from Thine infinite mercy. Amen.

Be merciful to us, O my God! Do not reject our prayers when, in the midst of our afflictions, we call upon Thy holy Name and seek with love and confidence Thy adorable Face. Amen.

We thank Thee, O Lord, for all Thy benefits, and we entreat Thee to engrave in our hearts feelings of love and of gratitude, putting upon our lips songs of thanksgiving to Thy eternal praise. Amen.

Shortly after the miracle of 1849 in Rome involving the Veil of Veronica, two linens of the replica engravings of the Veil of Veronica were sent to Leo Dupont from the Vatican. He gifted one of these engravings to a local adoration chapel and reverently displayed the other in his office. Beside the image, Leo always kept a burning oil lamp as a sign of reverence towards our Blessed Lord.

Many visitors would come to his office with different ailments. Leo Dupont would have them anoint themselves with the oil from his lamp and then say various prayers of reparation and petition. The miraculous healings started to occur, and the result was that over 6,000 documented miracles were reported. The miracles continued for 30 years! They became so numerous that Pope Pius IX declared Leo Dupont to be perhaps the greatest miracle worker in Church history.

The prayers that Leo Dupont would say before the venerated image of our Blessed Saviour were the prayers of healing, the Golden Arrow prayer and the Litany of the Holy Face.

Formulas which Leo Dupont used when anointing the sick with oil

In English: May the Lord himself deign, together with us, to anoint this sick person and to restore him to health. In the name of the Father, etc.

In Latin : Unctiones sanitatis conficiat et perficiat ipse Deus. In nomine Patris, etc.

In English: May the holy Names of Jesus, of Mary and of Joseph be known, blessed and glorified throughout the whole earth. Amen.

In Latin: Crux sacra, sit tibi lux et sanitas, benedictio et voluntas Domini nostri Jesu Christi. Amen.

Jesus, Mary, Joseph

Words of the Holy Face – Quotes from Our Blessed Lord and Sr. Marie de Saint-Pierre

Our Blessed Lord told Sr. Marie: "Rejoice, My Daughter, because the hour approaches when the most beautiful work under the sun will be born".

He made it known that all who honour His Holy Face will "shine with a brightness surpassing that of many others in eternal life."

Sister Marie wrote: "…after that He revealed to me that He wanted to give me a 'Golden Arrow' which would have the power of wounding Him delightfully, and which would also heal those other wounds inflicted by the malice of sinners, with torrents of graces emanating from it!".

"Just as in an earthly kingdom," Jesus stated, "money which is stamped with the picture of the sovereign or ruling executive of the country procures whatever one desires to purchase, so likewise in the Kingdom of Heaven, you shall obtain all that you desire by offering the coin of My precious Humanity which is my adorable Face".

Sister Marie stated, "Our Lord communicated to me that this time He would use as the instruments of punishment, not the elements, but 'the malice of revolutionary men'.

Our Blessed Lord told Sister Marie: "Oh, if you only knew their secret and diabolical plots and their anti-Christian principles! They are waiting for a favourable day in order to inflame the whole country. To obtain mercy, ask therefore that this Work of Reparation be established".

Sister Marie wrote: "He has commanded me to cross swords with the Communists who, as He told me, were sworn enemies of the Church, and of His Christ. He gave me to understand that the greatest number of these renegades were born in the bosom of the Church, of whom they now declare themselves the most bitter enemies…"

Our Blessed Lord said, "I hold you in my hands as an arrow; now I will shoot forth my arrow upon my enemies. To combat them, I give you the arms of my Passion, my Cross, of which they are enemies, as also to other instruments of my sufferings. Wage war against them with the simplicity of a child but with the courage of a valiant warrior. For this mission be signed with the blessing of the Father, and of the Son, and of the Holy Ghost".

"Think of the outrages inflicted on Me by the Society of Communists, the enemies of the Church and of her Christ! … They have laid their hands upon the anointed of the Lord. But their machinations are vain, their designs shall be foiled. I desire the establishment of the work of reparation! For it is the Work of Reparation to the Holy Face that will disarm God's justice."

Sister Marie stated, "The instruments which our Lord would use with which to punish the world would not be the elements but the malice of revolutionary men."

Our Blessed Lord said, "My Name is everywhere blasphemed! There are even children who blaspheme!"

"All those who honour my Face in a spirit of reparation will by so doing perform the act of the pious Veronica."

Sister Marie wrote: "Then He gave me, wonderful light on the sublimity of this Association and the preference with which He esteems it more than all others established in the Church, because of its object, to make reparation for all the outrages offered against the Divinity by blasphemy and by profanation of Sunday".

Our Blessed said to Sister Marie De Saint Pierre. "You cannot understand the malice and abomination of this sin. If my justice were not restrained by my mercy, it would instantly crush the guilty, and all creatures, even inanimate ones, would rise up to avenge my outraged honour."

After this, the Sister added, "He showed me the excellence of the Work of Reparation; how it surpasses all other devotions, is agreeable to God, to the angels, the saints, and is useful to the Church. Ah! If you knew the degree of glory you acquire in making but a single act of Reparation for blasphemy, in saying only once, in the spirit of Reparation, 'Admirable is the Name of God'!"

These passages were taken from the book titled - The Golden Arrow by Tan Books.

Twenty-Four Acts of Adoration

(For the Reparation of the Blasphemies Uttered During the Twenty-Four Hours of the Day)

Begin with the Magnificat (Luke 1: 46-55)

My soul proclaims the greatness of the Lord, and my spirit rejoices in God my Saviour, for He has looked with favour on his lowly servant. From this day all generations will call me blessed: the Almighty has done great things for me, and holy is His Name. He has mercy on those who fear Him in every generation. He has shown the strength of his arm. He has scattered the proud in their conceit. He has cast down the mighty from their thrones, and has lifted up the lowly. He has filled the hungry with good things, and the rich He has sent away empty. He has come to the help of His servant Israel, for He remembered His promise of mercy, the promise He made to our fathers, to Abraham and His children forever.

1. In union with the Sacred Heart of Jesus: *Come, let us adore the admirable Name of God which is above every name.*
2. In union with the holy heart of Mary: *Come, let us adore the admirable Name of God which is above every name.*

3. In union with the glorious Saint Joseph: *Come, let us adore the admirable Name of God which is above every name.*
4. In union with St. John the Baptist: *Come, let us adore the admirable Name of God which is above every name.*
5. In union with the choir of Seraphim: *Come let us adore the admirable Name of God which is above every name.*
6. In union with the choir of Cherubim: *Come let us adore the admirable Name of God, which is above every name.*
7. In union with the choir of Thrones: *Come let us adore the admirable Name of God, which is above every name.*
8. In union with the choir of Dominations: *Come let us adore the admirable Name of God which is above every name.*
9. In union with the choir of Virtues: *Come let us adore the admirable Name of God, which is above every name.*
10. In union with the choir of Powers: *Come let us adore the admirable Name of God, which is above every name.*
11. In union with the choir of Principalities: *Come let us adore the admirable Name of God, which is above every name.*
12. In union with the choir of Archangels: *Come let us adore the admirable Name of God which is above every name.*

13. In union with the choir of Angels: *Come let us adore the admirable Name of God which is above every name.*

14. In union with the seven Spirits which are before the throne of God and the twenty-four ancients: *Come let us adore the admirable Name of God which is above every name.*

15. In union with the choir of Patriarchs: *Come let us adore the admirable Name of God which is above every name.*

16. In union with the choir of Prophets: *Come let us adore the admirable Name of God, which is above every name.*

17. In union with the choir of the Apostles, and the four Evangelists: *Come let us adore the admirable Name of God which is above every name.*

18. In union with the choir of Martyrs: *Come let us adore the admirable Name of God which is above every name.*

19. In union with the choir of holy Pontiffs: *Come let us adore the admirable Name of God, which is above every name.*

20. In union with the choir of holy Confessors: *Come let us adore the admirable Name of God which is above every name.*

21. In union with the choir of holy Virgins: *Come let us adore the admirable Name of God, which is above every name.*

22. In union with the choir of holy Women: *Come let us adore the admirable Name of God, which is above every name.*

23. In union with all the heavenly Court: *Come let us adore the admirable Name of God, which is above every name.*

24. In union with the whole Church and in the name of all men: *Come, let us adore the admirable Name of God, which is above every name, and let us prostrate ourselves before it. Let us weep in the presence of the God who has made us, because He is the Lord our God; we are His people and the sheep which He Himself leads to His pastures. Amen.*

Prayers and Reflections of St. Augustine

I present myself before Thy Holy Face, O my Saviour, laden with my sins and the penalties which they have brought upon me. My sufferings are far less than what I deserve, for, although I am conscious of the just punishment of my sins, I do not, on that account, cease to commit fresh ones every day.

I am bowed down under Thy scourges, and I do not become better; my heart is full of bitterness, and my obstinacy, in doing evil, remains forever the same. My life passes away in misery, and I do not correct myself. When Thou hast chastised me, I make the best promises in the world; as soon as Thou liftest up Thy hand, I forget all that I promised Thee.

I make to Thee, O God! a sincere confession of my sins; I protest in Thy presence, that if Thou do not show mercy upon me, I shall be in danger of perishing utterly. Grant me, my Saviour, what I beg of Thee, although I do not deserve it, since Thou hast of Thy goodness drawn me out of nothingness to put me into a state wherein I can pray to Thee. Amen.

O Lord Jesus, let me know myself, let me know Thee, and desire nothing else but Thee.

Let me hate myself and love Thee, and do all things for the sake of Thee.

Let me humble myself and exalt Thee, and think of nothing else but Thee.

Let me die to myself and live in Thee, and take whatever happens as coming from Thee.

Let me forsake myself and walk after Thee, and ever desire to follow Thee.

Let me flee from myself and turn to Thee, that so I may merit to be defended by Thee.

Let me fear for myself, let me fear Thee, and be among those who are chosen by Thee.

Let me distrust myself and trust in Thee, and ever obey for the love of Thee.

Let me cleave to nothing but Thee, and ever be poor for the sake of Thee.

Look upon me that I may love Thee, call me that I may see Thee, and forever possess Thee. Amen.

"A single tear shed at the remembrance of the Passion of Jesus is worth more than a pilgrimage to Jerusalem, or a year of fasting on bread and water." ~ Saint Augustine

(The Following excerpt is taken from the book "The Holy Face in the Documents in the Church," Stefano Pedica, O.S.B.)

St. Augustine mentions the Lord's Holy Face so many times that it would merit a separate study. Jesus is beautiful, supremely beautiful: in Heaven, on the earth, in the womb of Mary, in the hands of relatives, beautiful in miracles, beautiful under the scourges. Suppose we should consider the Face of Jesus in the Passion. He is the example of humility and patience. Jesus, says the Saint, shows great and admirable patience in receiving the kiss of Judas. But is it not perhaps a greater and more excellent example of patience which Jesus gave in receiving and bearing the slap on His Sacred Countenance? He received it for our redemption, therefore Augustine finds therein motives of confidence in this pious prayer which he addresses to Jesus: "Be propitious, I pray Thee, and have pity on me, and turn not Thy Face from me, Thou who in redeeming me didst not turn Thy Face from those who insulted Thee, and spat upon Thee."

If we should consider the Face in its own nature, this predisposes it to the joy of the Beatific Vision.

St. Augustine's argument, therefore, is very strong, so to speak, which predisposes the final end to be the vision of God. Now, according to modern exegetists, the expression: "Facies Dei"-Face of God-does not always have the same significance in Holy Scripture. Augustine distinguishes sharply between "Face of God" and "Face of Christ".

The Face of God is the joy of the elect. The Face of Christ is the object of love and desire.

For what other object can we aspire towards than the Face of God - the truth? And elsewhere-the Face of God is the power by which He manifests Himself to the worthy, indeed to the just.

St. Augustine, like all the rest of the Holy Fathers, addresses Christ with the expressions of the Prophets and the Psalms, using at times indiscriminately the expression "Vultum Tuum" and "Faciem Tuam" straight to the Person of the Word, in the same manner that the word "Lord" Dominus refers to both the Father and the Son.

"Quaesivi vultum tuum" I have sought Thy Face. I have sought for Thee and none other beside Thee. Thy Face is my only reward. I will seek Thy Face, O Lord: in this demand will I persevere. Indeed, I will not look for any unworthy object, but only Thy Face that I may love Thee more generously, because I find none other more precious. The Face is the reward of the elect. The righteous shall dwell under Thine eyes, and when they will love Thy face, they will eat the bread of the sweat of their brow (Gen. 3, 19).

"Let us return, wiping away the sweat, let us end the weariness and the weeping that we may shine in Thy all-satisfying Face. Neither let us search anymore, because there is nothing better. Let us not abandon Thee, and we shall not be abandoned by Thee. Because what was said about the Lord, after the Resurrection? I will be filled with overflowing joy with Thy Face, because without Thy Face there would not be joy for us."

For St. Augustine, the Face of Christ is the symbol of the Beatific Vision. The significant passage concerning the Face of Christ to the Divine Essence in the Beatific Vision is easy to see oneself in the following words, which he uses to express the form of man and the form of God:

"He gave the human form to the pious and the weak (feeble in faith); to the pure and holy he reserved the form of God, so that we may be able to rejoice in Him and be happy for ever in His sight."

Prayers to the Holy Face by St. John Vianney

I salute You, I adore You, and I love You, oh adorable Face of my Beloved Jesus, as the noble stamp of the Divinity! Completely surrendering my soul to You, I most humbly beg You to stamp this seal upon us all, so that the Image of God may once more be reproduced by its imprint in our souls. Amen.

Oh, my beautiful Immaculate Mother Mary, Queen of Sorrows, I beg thee, by the inexpressible agony thou didst endure at the foot of the Cross, offer to the Eternal Father, in my stead, the Holy Face of Thy Divine Son, my Jesus, covered with blood, wounds, and other indignities heaped upon Him during His Sacred Passion, and beg of Him to grant (here mention the grace or favor you desire). Amen.

O Jesus, whose adorable Face was adored with profound respect by Mary and Joseph when they saw Thee for the first time, grant us the same grace in contemplating Thy Divine features.

Do not allow us ever to defile our souls by sin, but impress upon us the resemblance of Thy sufferings.

Send us a vivid remembrance of Thy Holy Face, so full of tears and pain, that we may never forget the infinite price of our redemption.

O merciful Advocate, have pity on us and on the whole world. Amen.

Prayers and Reflections from the Popes

Several Popes have spoken about the Holy Face devotion, highlighting its importance in understanding God's mercy and love and encouraging its practice as a means of reparation for sins. More than 30 Popes have expressed confidence in the authenticity of the Veil of Veronica and the Holy Shroud.

Blessings and indulgences have been placed by the Papal Magisterium on devotion to the Holy Face, never to be taken away due to the importance of this devotion.

Some Key Aspects of the Holy Face Devotion as Emphasized by the Popes:

Reparation for sins: The devotion is seen as a way to make amends for insults and offences against God, particularly those occurring publicly.

Understanding God's mercy: The Holy Face is a mirror reflecting God's infinite mercy and love.

Encounter with Christ: The devotion encourages a deeper encounter with Jesus, both in the Eucharist and in the suffering of others.

Imitation of Christ: Practicing the devotion involves imitating Christ's suffering, pain, and humiliation, uniting our own sufferings with his.

Eschatological dimension: The devotion connects the earthly suffering of Christ to the hope of eternal life and the final judgment.

Promotion of the Holy Face Devotion from Various Popes:

Pope Pius IX: Endorsed the devotion and said, "This salutary reparation to the Holy Face of Jesus is a divine work, destined to save modern society."

Pope Leo XIII: Established the Archconfraternity of the Holy Face, extending the devotion worldwide.

Pope Pius X: Expressed the desire that it be venerated in the homes of all Christian families.

Pope Pius XI: Gave pictures of the Holy Face from the Shroud to youths, saying: "They are the pictures of the Divine Son of Mary; they come, in fact, from that object known as the Shroud of Turin; still mysterious, but certainly not the work of any human hand."

Pope Pius XII: Asked to spread knowledge and veneration of so great and sacred a Relic. Established the Feast of the Holy Face on Shrove Tuesday before Ash Wednesday.

Pope John XXIII: On seeing the Relic, said, "This can only be the Lord's own doing."

Pope Paul VI: Praised the Holy Shroud, saying, "Perhaps only the Image from the Holy Shroud reveals to us something of the human and divine personality of Christ."

Pope Benedict XVI: Emphasized the devotion's three components: discipleship, the Eucharist, and its eschatological aspect, linking it to the suffering of the poor and the Passion of Christ.

Pope Francis: Referred to the Holy Face as the "Face of Mercy" and connected it to Divine Mercy Sunday.

Here are some prayers composed by some of the Popes regarding the Holy Face.

Prayer to the Holy Face by St. Pope John Paul II

Lord Jesus, Crucified and Risen; the image of the glory of the Father, Holy Face, which looks at us and searches for us, kind and merciful, You who call us to conversion and invite us to the fullness of love, we adore and bless you.

In your luminous Face, we learn to love and to be loved, to find freedom and reconciliation, to promote peace, which radiates from you and leads to you. In your glorified Face, we learn to overcome every form of egoism, to hope against every hope, to choose works of life against the actions of death.

Give us grace to place you at the centre of our life, to remain faithful amidst dangers and the changes of the world, to our Christian vocation; to announce to all people the power of the Cross and the Word which saves; to be watchful and active, to attend the needs of the little ones; to understand the need of true liberation, which had its beginning in you and will have its end in you.

Lord, grant to your Church to stand like your Virgin Mother, at the glorious Cross, and at the crosses of all people to bring about consolation, hope and comfort.

May the Holy Spirit, which you have granted, bring to maturation your work of salvation, through your Holy Face, which shines forever and ever. Amen.

St. John Paul II, "To contemplate the Face of Christ, and to contemplate it with Mary, is the program which I have set before the Church at the dawn of the third millennium..."

Lord Jesus, when I contemplate Your Face, the true image of the Father's glory, the sign of His mercy, the pledge of His love, I feel His presence. I feel You drawing me to love. Amen.

Prayer to the Holy Face by Pope Pius IX

O my Jesus! Cast upon us a look of mercy; turn Thy Face towards each one of us, even as Thou didst turn to Veronica, not that we may see it with the eyes of our body, for we do not deserve to do so, but turn it towards our hearts, that being sustained by Thee, we may ever draw from this powerful source, the vigor necessary to enable us to wage the combats we have to undergo. Amen.

Appendix IV:
The 100 Offerings of Our Lord
Jesus Christ to His Eternal Father

(Our Lord revealed to Sr. Marie de Saint Pierre this prayer was like building a wall of Protection.)

Thirty-Three Offerings of Jesus Christ in His Infancy and Hidden Life

1. Eternal Father, I offer Thee Jesus, Incarnate in the womb of the Virgin Mary for the salvation of men.
2. Eternal Father, I offer Thee Jesus, sanctifying St. John the Baptist in the womb of His mother, St. Elizabeth.
3. Eternal Father, I offer Thee Jesus, a captive for nine months in the chaste womb of His Blessed Mother.
4. Eternal Father, I offer Thee Jesus, rejected by the inhabitants of Bethlehem.
5. Eternal Father, I offer Thee Jesus, coming forth from the womb of His Mother and born in a poor stable.
6. Eternal Father, I offer Thee Jesus, wrapped in swaddling-clothes and laid in a manger.

7. Eternal Father, I offer Thee Jesus, trembling with cold and warmed by the breath of an ox and a donkey.
8. Eternal Father, I offer Thee Jesus, weeping for our sins in the manger.
9. Eternal Father, I offer Thee Jesus, by the hands of Mary and St. Joseph, for the salvation of the world.
10. Eternal Father, I offer Thee Jesus, nursed by Mary.
11. Eternal Father, I offer Thee Jesus, adored by angels in the stable of Bethlehem.
12. Eternal Father, I offer Thee Jesus, adored by the poor shepherds.
13. Eternal Father, I offer Thee Jesus, circumcised and named Jesus, beginning to fulfill the office of Saviour in offering Thee the first-fruits of His Blood.
14. Eternal Father, I offer Thee Jesus, receiving the gifts and adorations of the Magi.
15. Eternal Father, I offer Thee all the glory that Jesus has rendered Thee during the forty days He dwelt in the stable of Bethlehem.
16. Eternal Father, I offer Thee Jesus, brought to the Temple by Mary and Joseph, and received with great joy by the holy old man Simeon and the prophetess Anna.
17. Eternal Father, I offer Thee Jesus, who offers Himself to Thy Divine justice to be the repairer of Thy outraged glory and the holy victim of sinners.

18. Eternal Father, I offer Thee Jesus, fleeing into Egypt to avoid the murderous hand of Herod.
19. Eternal Father, I offer Thee Jesus, poor and unknown in His exile, but tenderly loved and profoundly adored by Mary, Joseph, and the angels.
20. Eternal Father, I offer Thee Jesus, carried in the arms of Mary and Joseph and submitting to all the trials of infancy.
21. Eternal Father, I offer Thee Jesus, nursed by His Divine Mother for fifteen months.
22. Eternal Father, I offer Thee the first steps, the first words, the first actions of Thy Divine Son Jesus.
23. Eternal Father, I offer Thee all that Jesus suffered the seven years of His exile in Egypt.
24. Eternal Father, I offer Thee Jesus, returning to Nazareth between Mary and Joseph.
25. Eternal Father, I offer Thee Jesus, growing in age and in wisdom before God and men.
26. Eternal Father, I offer Thee Jesus, conducted to the Temple at the age of twelve years to celebrate the Passover.
27. Eternal Father, I offer Thee Jesus, remaining three days in the Temple in the midst of the Doctors of the Law, and filling them with admiration.
28. Eternal Father, I offer Thee Jesus, found by Mary and Joseph, returning to Nazareth, and being perfectly submissive to them.

29. Eternal Father, I offer Thee Jesus, hiding His glory in the workshop of St. Joseph, and seeming to be only a carpenter.
30. Eternal Father, I offer Thee Jesus, working for His support by the sweat of His brow.
31. Eternal Father, I offer Thee Jesus, assisting St. Joseph during His last illness and at the hour of His death.
32. Eternal Father, I offer Thee Jesus, consoling Mary, His Blessed Mother, for the death of her holy spouse.
33. Eternal Father, I offer Thee all the glory that Jesus has rendered Thee during the thirty years of His hidden and laborious life, also all the merits He has acquired for us.

Eternal Father, I offer Thee all the glory that our Divine Saviour Jesus has rendered Thee during the thirty years of His hidden and laborious life, and all the merits He has acquired for us from the moment of His Divine Incarnation until His evangelical Life. I make this offering for the honour and glory of Thy Holy Name, in reparation for the indignities offered our Saviour; finally, for the wants of the Holy Church, the Salvation of France (or the country you are praying for), and the Work of Reparation.

Thirty-Three Offerings of Jesus in His Evangelical Life

1. Eternal Father, I offer Thee Jesus, baptized in the river Jordan by St. John the Baptist.
2. Eternal Father, I offer Thee Jesus, led by the Spirit into the desert, and suffering their hunger and thirst.
3. Eternal Father, I offer Thee Jesus, spending His nights in the desert among wild beasts.
4. Eternal Father, I offer Thee Jesus, passing days and nights in prayer, watering the ground with His Divine tears, in expiation for our sins.
5. Eternal Father, I offer Thee Jesus, tempted by the evil spirit to change stones into bread.
6. Eternal Father, I offer Thee Jesus, carried by Satan to the top of the Temple, and tempted by this evil spirit to cast Himself down.
7. Eternal Father, I offer Thee Jesus, carried by Satan to the top of a high mountain, with the promise of all the kingdoms of the world.
8. Eternal Father, I offer Thee Jesus, triumphing over the temptations of the evil spirit and confronting him with the words of Holy Scripture.
9. Eternal Father, I offer Thee Jesus, in the desert, taking the food ministered by the angels.

10. Eternal Father, I offer Thee all the glory that Jesus has rendered Thee in the desert and all the merits He has acquired for us.

11. Eternal Father, I offer Thee Jesus, coming forth from the desert and going to make known to His Blessed Mother the mission He was about to commence.

12. Eternal Father, I offer Thee Jesus, choosing poor fishermen for His Apostles.

13. Eternal Father, I offer Thee Jesus, going from city to city, from town to town, preaching everywhere the Kingdom of God, and making known His Divine Father.

14. Eternal Father, I offer Thee Jesus, followed by immense crowds, even to the desert.

15. Eternal Father, I offer Thee Jesus, multiplying the loaves and fishes to feed the multitude.

16. Eternal Father, I offer Thee Jesus, consoling the afflicted.

17. Eternal Father, I offer Thee Jesus, curing the sick and raising the dead.

18. Eternal Father, I offer Thee Jesus, driving out the evil spirit from those who were possessed.

19. Eternal Father, I offer Thee Jesus, giving sight to the blind and hearing to the deaf.

20. Eternal Father, I offer Thee Jesus, curing the lame and making the dumb to speak.

21. Eternal Father, I offer Thee Jesus, converting sinners and doing good to all.
22. Eternal Father, I offer Thee Jesus, weeping for the death of Lazarus and raising Him to life.
23. Eternal Father, I offer Thee Jesus, converting Mary Magdalene.
24. Eternal Father, I offer Thee Jesus, weary by the wayside and seated on Jacob's Well.
25. Eternal Father, I offer Thee Jesus, asking drink of the Samaritan woman, converting her, and making known to her that He was the promised Messiah.
26. Eternal Father, I offer Thee Jesus, confounding His enemies with an admirable wisdom when they presented before Him a woman taken in adultery.
27. Eternal Father, I offer Thee Jesus, driving the sellers out of the Temple.
28. Eternal Father, I offer Thee Jesus, transfigured on Mt. Tabor, conversing with Moses and Elias on the greatness of the sorrows of His Passion.
29. Eternal Father, I offer Thee Jesus, embracing and blessing little children, bidding us to become as one of them to enter the Kingdom of Heaven.
30. Eternal Father, I offer Thee Jesus, entering the city of Jerusalem in triumph, and received as a King by the people.
31. Eternal Father, I offer Thee Jesus, weeping for the sins of Jerusalem.

32. Eternal Father, I offer Thee Jesus alone and abandoned, obliged on the evening of the Feast to seek the hospitality of Martha and Mary, at Bethany.
33. Eternal Father, I offer Thee all the glory that Jesus has rendered Thee during the three years of His Divine preachings.

Eternal Father, I offer Thee all the glory that Jesus, our Divine Saviour, has rendered Thee, all the infinite merits He has acquired for us from the moment of His evangelical life until His Passion. I make this offering for the honour and glory of Thy Holy Name, to repair the outrages offered our Divine Saviour; finally, for the wants of the Holy Church, the salvation of France (or country you are praying for), and the extension of the Work of Reparation.

Thirty-Four Offerings of Jesus in His Suffering and Glorious Life

1. Eternal Father, I offer Thee Jesus, sold for thirty pieces of silver by the traitor Judas.
2. Eternal Father, I offer Thee Jesus, taking His Last Supper with His Apostles.
3. Eternal Father, I offer Thee Jesus, humbling Himself unto washing the feet of His Apostles.
4. Eternal Father, I offer Thee Jesus, instituting the adorable Sacrament of the Eucharist and ordaining His Apostles priests of the New Law.
5. Eternal Father, I offer Thee Jesus, praying and in agony in the Garden of Olives.
6. Eternal Father, I offer Thee Jesus, suffering in His Divine Heart, all the sorrows of His Passion and watering the earth with a profuse sweat of blood.
7. Eternal Father, I offer Thee Jesus, sorrowful unto death in the Garden of Olives, burdened with all the sins of the world, and accepting the chalice from Thy Hand.
8. Eternal Father, I offer Thee Jesus, betrayed and kissed by the perfidious Judas, delivering Himself up to His enemies to be bound and blindfolded for our sins.
9. Eternal Father, I offer Thee Jesus, abandoned by His disciples, maltreated and outraged by the

soldiers, and led to the house of the high-priest Annas.

10. Eternal Father, I offer Thee Jesus, interrogated and receiving a blow from a servant.

11. Eternal Father, I offer Thee Jesus, conducted to the house of Caiaphas and accused by false witnesses.

12. Eternal Father, I offer Thee Jesus, treated as a blasphemer because He declared to His enemies that He was the Son of God.

13. Eternal Father, I offer Thee Jesus, despised, struck, and spit upon during that horrible night, and treated as the vilest slave.

14. Eternal Father, I offer Thee Jesus, conducted in chains to Pilate's house.

15. Eternal Father, I offer Thee Jesus, led to the court of Herod and despised by that impious king.

16. Eternal Father, I offer Thee Jesus, reconducted to the house of Pilate, treated with contempt and humiliation on the streets of Jerusalem by a nation which He had overwhelmed with benefits.

17. Eternal Father, I offer Thee Jesus, tied to the column and torn by the stripes of the scourge.

18. Eternal Father, I offer Thee Jesus, covered with wounds and blood, trampled upon by His executioners.

19. Eternal Father, I offer Thee Jesus, arrayed as a mock-king, crowned with thorns, robed in a scarlet

mantle, His arms tied, and a reed for a sceptre in His hand.

20. Eternal Father, I offer Thee Jesus, outraged, despised, and then shown to the people.

21. Eternal Father, I offer Thee Jesus, rejected by His people, who with loud voices demanded His death and preferred to Him an infamous thief, Barabbas.

22. Eternal Father, I offer Thee Jesus, condemned by Pilate to the death of the Cross.

23. Eternal Father, I offer Thee Jesus, given over to an insolent multitude, who vent upon this sweet Lamb, so meek and humble of Heart, all that the darkest malice could devise.

24. Eternal Father, I offer Thee Jesus, going forth from Pilate's Hall between the two thieves, carrying the Cross upon His Divine Shoulders, bruised and bleeding.

25. Eternal Father, I offer Thee Jesus, exhausted by fatigue, falling several times under the heavy burden of His Cross, beaten and overwhelmed with injurious treatment by His executioners.

26. Eternal Father, I offer Thee Jesus on the summit of Calvary, despoiled of His garments and extending Himself on the tree of the Cross as a Lamb without stain.

27. Eternal Father, I offer Thee Jesus, nailed with heavy blows of the hammer to the Cross.

28. Eternal Father, I offer Thee Jesus, suspended for three hours between heaven and earth, satiated with revilings, partaking of gall and vinegar, and tasting with delight the intensity of interior and exterior sufferings.
29. Eternal Father, I offer Thee Jesus, asking forgiveness for His executioners, granting pardon to the good thief, and giving us His most Blessed Mother.
30. Eternal Father, I offer Thee Jesus, consummating His sacrifice and yielding up His Holy Soul into Thy Hands, uttering a loud cry to call all sinners to Him, inclining His Head to give them the kiss of peace and the last sigh of His Heart.
31. Eternal Father, I offer Thee Jesus, His Heart pierced by a lance, His Sacred Body covered with wounds and blood, taken down from the Cross and placed in the arms of His Divine Mother.
32. Eternal Father, I offer Thee Jesus, embalmed and shrouded by His Holy Mother, assisted by His faithful friends; then carried to the sepulchre and remaining therein three days, as He had foretold.
33. Eternal Father, I offer Thee Jesus, rising victorious from the tomb and visiting His Blessed Mother.
34. Eternal Father, I offer Thee Jesus, appearing to His Apostles and the holy women for their consolation and instruction, gloriously ascending to heaven in their presence forty days after His Resurrection.

Eternal Father, I offer Thee all the glory that Jesus Christ, our Divine Saviour, has rendered Thee, as well as all the merits He has acquired for us during His sorrowful and glorious life. I make this offering for the honour and glory of Thy Holy Name, in reparation for the indignities offered to our Saviour — in fine, for the needs of the Holy Church, for the salvation of France (or the country you are praying for) and the entire world, and for the extension of the Work of Reparation.

This is My well-beloved Son, in whom I am well pleased. Hear ye Him. In truth, I say to thee that all thou wilt ask the Father in My Name He will grant. Ask, and thou shalt receive.

Our Lord gave me to behold a mysterious wall protecting France against the arrow of divine justice. He gave me to understand that this wall, which reached up to Heaven, was the exercise which I practiced each day, joined no doubt to the prayers and merits offered to God by so many souls for the salvation of France. This exercise consists in presenting the Face of Jesus a Hundred to His Father, in honour of all mysteries of the life and death of the Divine Saviour and in offering these merits of each of these mysteries for the Salvation of France. (Sister Marie de Saint Pierre)

Loving Aspiration to our Blessed Lord
to Repair Against Blasphemy

O Jesus, eternal truth and wisdom, who wast called a tempter and a madman, *I adore thee and love thee with all my heart.*

O Jesus, in whom dwelt all the riches of divine science, who wast looked upon as ignorant and as the son of a carpenter, I adore thee, etc.

O Jesus, source of life, who didst hear the Jews say of thee," Will he kill himself? " Because thou saidst,' I go where thou canst not follow me,' I adore thee, etc.

O Jesus, Divine Word, who wast supposed to be possessed by a devil and wast called a Samaritan, I adore thee, etc.

O Jesus, God thrice holy, who wast treated as a sinner by the High-Priests, I adore thee, etc.

O Jesus, model of sobriety, whose enemies accused thee of gluttony, I adore thee, etc.

O Jesus, enemy of sin, but full of pity for the guilty, who wast called the friend of publicans and sinners, I adore thee, etc.

O Jesus, the splendour of the Father and the image of his substance, who wast accused of being a false prophet, I adore thee, etc.

O Jesus, the enemy of falsehood, who didst hear the Jews cast doubts on thy words by saying with irony, "Thou art not yet fifty and hast seen Abraham?" I adore thee, etc.

O Jesus, all-powerful God, who, to conform with our nature, which thou hadst taken upon thyself, wished to hide and go from the Temple, that thou mightest not be stoned by thine enemies, I adore thee, etc.

O Jesus, only Son and faithful worshipper of the living God, who wast accused by the High-Priest of blasphemy and wast adjudged worthy of death, I adore thee, etc.

O Jesus, King of glory, who, full of sweetness and humility, didst permit thy Face to be spat upon, thy Head to be covered with a veil and beaten and bruised, I adore thee, etc.

O Jesus, who dost fathom our hearts and loins, to whom nothing is hidden, and who didst suffer without complaint these insolent words, "If thou art the Christ, tell who has struck thee," I adore thee, etc.

O Jesus, King of peace, accused of perverting the nation and preventing the payment of the tribute-money, of causing the people to revolt and calling thyself King and Messiah, I adore thee, etc.

O Jesus, King of kings, scorned by Herod and his court, and dressed in derision in a white robe like a madman, I adore thee, etc.

O Jesus, full of love, who didst hear the cry of the people, "Let this one die, and restore Barabbas to us," "Let his blood be upon us and upon our children," I adore thee, etc.

O Jesus, King of heaven and earth, crowned with thorns, shamefully beaten, and so cruelly outraged by these words," We salute thee, O King of the Jews," I adore thee, etc. O Jesus, of infinite bounty, principle of all being, Sovereign Master of the world, who didst hear these words of doom," Crucify him, crucify him, lead him away! Lead him away! We have no other king but Caesar," I adore thee, etc.

O Jesus, worthy of all praise, who when upon the Cross wast blasphemed by the passers-by, the impenitent thief, the High Priests, the elders of the people, and the scribes and soldiers, I adore thee, etc.

O Jesus, holy victim of sinners, who didst hear thine enemies say to thee," He saved others and cannot save himself; let this Christ, this King of Israel, now come down from the Cross, that we may see and believe in him," I adore thee, etc. O Jesus, full of confidence, love, and respect for thy Divine Father, who wast wounded with the most lively pain when they said on seeing thee die, " He puts his trust in God; if God love him let him deliver him now, for he has said, I am the Son of God," I adore thee, and I love thee with all my heart.

Prayer:

I bitterly compassionate, O my Saviour, Jesus Christ, the anguish endured by thy divine Heart when thou didst hear blasphemies that thine enemies poured forth against thee and thy heavenly Father; but what, O Jesus, must be thy sorrow in seeing that after thou hast given thy life, and the last drop of thy blood, for the salvation of men, thou shouldst still have, after the lapse of centuries, new enemies who reiterate a thousand times these blasphemies! Accept, my sweet Jesus, the ardent desire we have to repair all the outrages and scorn thou hast received, and still dost receive every day, from heretics and the impious. Oh! Why cannot we protect thee from the anger of those that hate thee, and who are leagued against thee and thy Holy Church, thy stainless spouse? Repeat with us, O merciful Jesus, that touching prayer thou didst offer to thy Divine Father before breathing thy last sigh:" Forgive them, Father, for they know not what they do!" We offer thee, as reparation for the many offences against thee, all the glory, honour, and praise, and all the joy that the Holy Virgin and St. Joseph, the Saints and elect, did give thee and will ever give thee in time and eternity. Amen.

Offering of the Infinite Merits of Our Lord Jesus Christ to His Eternal Father in Order to Appease the Divine Justice and Draw Down Mercy on the Country

Eternal Father, turn Thine offended eyes from the culpable (*Country*), whose face has become hideous in Thy eyes, and look upon the Face of Thy Son which we offer thee – this well-beloved Son, in whom Thou art well pleased. Listen, we beseech Thee, to the voice of His blood and His wounds, which cry out for mercy.

Eternal Father, behold the Incarnation of Jesus, Thy Divine Son, and His sojourn in the womb of His Blessed Mother. We offer this to Thee for the honour and glory of Thy Holy Name and for the salvation of the (*Country*).

Eternal Father, behold the birth of Jesus in the stable of Bethlehem and the mysteries of His most Holy Infancy. We offer them to Thee, etc.

Eternal Father, behold the crib, the swaddling bands which have served Jesus at His birth. We offer them to Thee, etc.

Eternal Father, behold the poor, hidden, and laborious life of Jesus at Nazareth. We offer it to Thee, etc.

Eternal Father, behold the baptism of Jesus and His forty days' retreat in the desert. We offer these to Thee, etc.

Eternal Father, behold the journeys, the vigils, the prayers, the miracles, and sermons of Jesus. We offer them to Thee, etc.

Eternal Father, behold the Last Supper which Jesus made with His disciples, at which He washed their feet and instituted the august sacrament of the Eucharist. We offer it to Thee, etc.

Eternal Father, behold the agony of Jesus in the Garden of Olives, the sweat of blood which covered His Body and flowed to the ground. We offer this to Thee, etc.

Eternal Father, behold the outrages which Jesus received before His judges, and His condemnation to death. We offer them to Thee, etc.

Eternal Father, behold Jesus, burdened with His Cross and walking towards the place where He is to be immolated. We offer Him to Thee, etc.

Eternal Father, behold Jesus crucified between two thieves, tasting gall and vinegar, blasphemed, and dying to repair Thy glory and to save the world. We offer Him to Thee, etc.

Eternal Father, behold the Sacred head of Jesus crowned with thorns. We offer it to Thee, etc.

Eternal Father, behold the adorable Face of Jesus bruised with buffets, covered with sweat, dust, and blood. We offer it to Thee, etc.

Eternal Father, behold the adorable Body of Jesus taken down from the Cross. We offer it to Thee, etc.

Eternal Father, behold the Heart, Soul, and Divinity of Jesus, this Holy Victim who in dying has triumphed over sin. We offer them to Thee, etc.

Eternal Father, behold all that Jesus Christ, Thy only Son, has done during the thirty-three years of His mortal life to accomplish the work of our Redemption. Behold all the mysteries of His Holy Life. We offer them to Thee, etc.

Eternal Father, behold all the desires, all the thoughts, words, actions, virtues, perfections, and prayers of Jesus Christ, also all His sufferings and humiliations. We offer them to Thee, etc.

Eternal Father, behold the Cross, the nails, the crown of thorns, the reed, the bloody scourge, the column, the lance, the sepulchre, the winding-sheet, and all the instruments which were used in the Passion of Jesus, Thy Divine Son. We offer them to Thee, etc.

Crown to the Glory of the Holy Name of God

On an ordinary Rosary, this is a beautiful little Chaplet to the sacred Name of God through the Heart of Jesus in the most Holy Sacrament.

Instead of the Credo, say:

We adore Thee, O Jesus, and we bless Thee, because Thou hast redeemed the world by Thy holy Cross.

Upon the three small beads of the cross, say:

May the most Holy Name of God be glorified by the most holy soul of the incarnate Word.

May the Most Sacred Name of God be glorified by the sacred Heart of the incarnate Word.

May the most adorable Name of God be glorified by all the wounds of the incarnate Word.

Upon the five large beads, say:

We invoke Thee, O sacred Name of the living God, by the mouth of Jesus in the most holy Sacrament, and we offer Thee, O my God, by the blessed hands of the most holy Virgin Mary, all the holy hosts which are upon our altars as a sacrifice of honorable amends and of reparation for all the blasphemies which outrage Thy Holy Name.

Upon each small bead of the ten, say:

1. Hail, O sacred Name of the living God, through the Heart of Jesus in the most Holy Sacrament.
2. I revere Thee, O sacred Name of the living God, through the Heart of Jesus in the most Holy Sacrament.
3. I adore Thee, O sacred Name of the living God, through the Heart of Jesus in the most Holy Sacrament.
4. I glorify Thee, O sacred Name of the living God, through the Heart of Jesus in the most Holy Sacrament.
5. I praise Thee, O sacred Name of the living God, through the Heart of Jesus in the most Holy Sacrament.
6. I admire Thee, O sacred Name of the living God, through the Heart of Jesus in the most Holy Sacrament.
7. I celebrate Thee, O sacred Name of the living God, through the Heart of Jesus in the most Holy Sacrament.
8. I exalt Thee, O sacred Name of the living God, through the Heart of Jesus in the most Holy Sacrament.
9. I love Thee, O sacred Name of the living God, through the Heart of Jesus in the most Holy Sacrament.

10. I bless Thee, O sacred Name of the living God, through the Heart of Jesus in the most Holy Sacrament.

We invoke Thee, O sacred Name of the living God, through the mouth of Jesus in the most Holy Sacrament, and we offer Thee, o my God, by the blessed hands of the most holy Virgin Mary, all the Holy Hosts which are upon our altars, as a sacrifice of honorable amends for all the blasphemies which outrage Thy Holy Name.

Praises of the Holy Face

Blessed be Jesus!

Blessed be the Holy Face of Jesus!

Blessed be the Holy Face in the majesty and beauty of Its heavenly features!

Blessed be the Holy Face through the words which issued from Its Divine mouth!

Blessed be the Holy Face through all the glances which escaped from Its adorable eyes!

Blessed be the Holy Face in the Transfiguration of Tabor!

Blessed be the Holy Face in the fatigues of Its apostolate!

Blessed be the Holy Face in the bloody sweat of the agony!

Blessed be the Holy Face in the humiliations of the Passion!

Blessed be the Holy Face in the sufferings of death!

Blessed be the Holy Face in the splendour of the Resurrection!

Blessed be the Holy Face in the glory of light eternal!

Praises to the Name of God

Blessed be God.

Blessed be His Holy Name.

Blessed be Jesus Christ, true God and true Man.

Blessed be the Name of Jesus.

Blessed be His Most Sacred Heart.

Blessed be His Most Precious Blood.

Blessed be Jesus in the Most Holy Sacrament of the Altar.

Blessed be the Holy Spirit, the Paraclete.

Blessed be the great Mother of God, Mary most holy.

Blessed be her holy and Immaculate Conception.

Blessed be her glorious Assumption.

Blessed be the name of Mary, Virgin and Mother.

Blessed be St. Joseph, her most chaste Spouse.

Blessed be God in His Angels and in His Saints.

Consecration of Ourselves to the Holy Face

Oh, adorable Face of my Jesus, humbly prostrate in Thy divine presence, I desire to consecrate myself wholly to Thee and henceforth to live only for Thee. Why have I not at my disposal the hearts of all creatures, in order to offer them up as a holocaust to Thee? Alas! Oh well beloved Face, I have only my own, unworthy as it is of Thy attention and often rebelling against the movements of Thy grace; nevertheless, I give it to Thee, my poor heart, and I consecrate it to Thee, in order that, from this moment and during all the days of my life, it may be inflamed with the holy ardour of Thy divine love. Purify it, warm it with the blessed rays of Thy eternal light, so that I may henceforth exclaim with the prophet king: "Lord, the light of Thy Face is engraved upon us; Thou hast caused joy to spring forth in my heart." (Ps. 4: 7.)

I offer Thee then this day, deliberately and with great joy, the sacrifice of all the delights which may be offered me on earth. Accept, oh adorable Face, oh Thou whom I love more than aught else in the world, accept the homage of myself, which I present to Thee at this moment. I thrill with gladness and with love, whilst thus consecrating to Thee the whole of my being. Yes, I offer and consecrate to Thee my heart, my body, my soul, my spirit, and my life; my heart, to love only Thee, O beauty ever ancient and ever new; my body, to serve as an instrument of reparation and of all that belongs to Thy glory; my soul, to reflect unceasingly the image of Thy different graces; my spirit, to think only upon Thee, and upon all that will tend to spread devotion to Thee; my life, my whole life, in order that it may be penetrated with Thy sweet memory, and filled with actions worthy Thy Name, so that I may one day merit that life eternal, in which, according to the expression of Thy apostle, I may contemplate Thee, no longer as in an enigma and through a mirror, but face to face, and as Thou art. Whilst waiting until His supreme grace shall be accorded to me, O Holy Face of Jesus, make me walk here below in the light of Thy benign eyes, that when I shall appear before Thee, Thou mayest name me by my name, Thou mayest kiss me with the kiss of Thy mouth, and Thou mayest introduce me into the immortal society of the blessed who are occupied without ceasing in contemplating Thee, praising Thee, adoring Thee, and eternally singing Thy mercies. Amen.

Appendix V:
Prayers of Reparation

Prayer to Entreat for the Triumph of the Church by Means of the Holy Face

Taken from the Scriptures (Daniel 9: 13, 14, 17, 18, 19)

Lord, we entreated not Thy Face that we might turn from our iniquities and think on Thy truth. And the Lord hath watched upon the evil, and hath brought it upon us: the Lord our God is just in all his works which he hath done: for we have not hearkened to His voice.

Now, therefore, O our God, hear the supplication of Thy servant, and his prayers: and shew Thy Face upon Thy sanctuary which is desolate, for Thy own sake. Incline, O my God, Thy ear, and hear; open Thy eyes, and see our desolation, and the city upon which Thy Name is called: for it is not for our justifications that we present our prayers before Thy Face, but for the multitude of Thy tender mercies.

O Lord, hear: O Lord, be appeased: hearken and do: delay not for Thy own sake, O my God: because Thy Name is invocated upon Thy city, and upon Thy people. But, there is no one who invokes this powerful Name; there is none who lifts himself up to Thee, and who endeavours by his supplications to restrain the effects of Thy anger. Therefore, Thou hast turned away Thy Face from us, and Thou hast bruised us under the weight of our iniquities.

Lord, look upon us in pity, keep no longer silence, and do not leave us prey to such sharp sorrows.

Oh! If Thou wouldst open the heavens and come down! The mountains would tremble before Thy Face. Thy Name would be known amongst Thy enemies, the nations would be struck with terror. Cast Thy eyes upon us, and remember that we are Thy people. Amen.

Act of Reparation for all the Outrages Which Jesus Christ Suffered in His Holy Face

I adore Thee, and I praise Thee, O my divine Jesus, Son of the living God, for all the outrages Thou hast endured for me, who am the most miserable of Thy creatures, in all the sacred members of Thy body, but especially in the most noble part of Thyself, that is to say, in Thy Face.

I salute Thee, amiable Face, wounded with blows and scourges, soiled with spittle and disfigured by the evil treatment which the impious Jews caused Thee to suffer.

I salute you, O lovely eyes! All bathed in the tears you have shed for our salvation.

I salute you, sacred ears, tormented by an infinity of blasphemies, injuries and shameful mockings.

I salute you, O holy mouth! Filled with grace and sweetness towards sinners and made to drink of vinegar and gall by the monstrous ingratitude of those whom Thou hadst chosen to be Thy people.

In reparation for all these ignominies, I offer Thee all the homage which has been rendered Thee in the holy place where Thou hast willed to be honoured by the special devotion to which I unite myself with my whole heart. Amen.

Prayer of Reparation: To the Outraged Divinity of Our Lord Jesus Christ

O Lord Jesus, after contemplating Thy features, disfigured by anguish, and after meditating upon Thy Passion, how can my heart not be consumed with love for Thee, and hatred for those sins which, even at this day, wound Thy adorable Face? Permit me not, O Lord! to feel merely compassion alone; make of me a worthy child of Mary, and accord me the grace, as Thou didst to Thy divine Mother, to follow Thee so closely on this new Calvary, that the insults destined for Thee, O Jesus! May fall upon me, a member of Thy Holy Church and cause me to undertake with courage the duty of expiation and of love. Amen.

Act of Love to the Holy Face

Adorable Face of my Jesus, my only love, my light and my life, grant that I may see no one except Thee, that I may know no one except Thee, that I may love Thee alone, that I may live with Thee, of Thee, by Thee, and for Thee. Amen.

Act of Reparation

O well-beloved Face of Jesus! Humbly prostrate in Thy presence, we adore Thee for those who refuse to adore Thee; we love Thee and we pray to Thee, for those who refuse to love Thee and who blaspheme Thee. Unhappy madmen! If they knew Thee better, with what repentance and confusion would they turn towards Thee, how they would seek to make compensation to Thee for all which Thou hast suffered for them!

The audacity of impiety has increased; a clamour issuing from hell has been raised for the purpose of denying Thy divinity and outraging the Church, a diabolical pact has been formed against God and against his Christ. It is for us, faithful Christians, to close our ranks under the banner of the Holy Face, to multiply our phalanx of reparation, to offer to Jesus, as did Veronica, the veil of our love and of our veneration. We need no longer, O merciful Face, envy the happiness of that heroic woman; by a redoublement of faith, of fervour and of zeal, we may, like her, wipe Thy tears away, staunch Thy blood, and solace Thy sufferings.

O sacred Face! Permit us to weep over the crimes of our erring brethren. Enable us to repair, by our sighs and our love, the attempts made against Thy divinity. Ah! We attest that divinity which has its habitation in Thee, with our whole heart; and if, in order to maintain it, the sacrifice of our life were necessary, we would joyously make an offering of it to Thee.

O well beloved Face! Let Thy eyes of mercy and compassion rest upon us. Pardon this deicidal century, which refuses to bend its proud head to Thy sovereign authority. Dissipate, by the light of Thy presence, the darkness which envelopes us, and which, if it were not for Thee, would drag us down into the still deeper darkness of death. Convert the blasphemers, bring back to the light of faith the ignorant and incredulous, console the just, strengthen the weak, and grant that all, with one accent of faith and love, may exclaim with the Prophet; "Now, Lord, we follow Thee with our whole heart, we fear Thee and we seek after Thy adorable Face." (Dan. III, 41.)

An Act of Honourable Amends

To The Most Holy Face of Our Lord Jesus Christ, In Reparation of The Sin of Blasphemy, Of the Profanation of Sundays, And of Other Impious Crimes Against God and The Church. To Be Recited Publicly' At the Monthly Meetings of the Archconfraternity

Most holy and most adorable Face of the Saviour, humbly prostrate in Thy presence, we present ourselves before Thee, in order, by a solemn act of faith and of piety, to render Thee the homage of veneration, praise and love which is Thy due. We also desire to offer to Thee honourable amends and a public reparation for the sins, blasphemies and sacrileges of which the present generation has rendered itself culpable towards The Divine Majesty, and which, regarding Thee, oh well beloved Face, renew the ignominies and the sufferings of Thy Passion.

It is with terror and profound affliction that we are witnesses of these monstrous crimes, which cannot fail to draw down upon society and upon our families, the malediction and the chastisements of divine justice. We see, in fact, all around us the law of the Lord and the authority of His Church despised and trodden under foot; His thrice holy Name denied or blasphemed, the Sunday which he has reserved for his worship, publicly profaned; his altars and his offices forsaken for criminal or frivolous pleasures. Impious sectarians attack all that is sacred and religious. But it is, above all, the Divinity of Christ, the Son of the living God; it is the Incarnate Word; it is the august Face and the Crucifix which They attack with the greatest fury; the spit and the blows of the Jews are renewed by the insults and the outrages which their hatred dares, in every possible manner, to inflict upon Thee, oh Face full of sweetness and of love.

Pardon, a thousand times pardon, for all these crimes! May we make amends for them by our humble supplications and the fervour of our homage! But guilty and sinners as we are, what can we offer the Eternal Father in order to appease his just anger, if it be not Thyself, oh sorrowful Face, who has deigned to make Thyself our advocate and our victim? Supply what may be wanting in us by Thy satisfactions and Thy merits.

Heavenly Father, we entreat Thee, « Look on the Face of Thy Christ. » Behold the wounds which disfigure it, the tears which escape from its sunken eyes; the sweat with which it is bathed; the blood which flows in streams down its profaned and wounded cheeks. Behold also its invincible patience, its unalterable gentleness, its infinite tenderness and its merciful goodness towards sinners. This Holy Face is turned towards Thee, and, before exhaling its last sigh, lovingly inclined upon the Cross, it implores Thee in favour of those who curse and outrage it. Oh Father, listen to that suppliant cry, permit thyself to be touched; have pity on us and pardon us. Grant, moreover, that in the presence of this divine Face, equally formidable and powerful, the enemies of Thy Name may take flight and disappear; that they may be converted and live!

Lord, show us Thy Face, and we shall be saved.

Amen! Amen!

Prayer to Offer the Holy Face of Jesus to God the Father to Appease His Justice and Draw Down Mercy Upon Us

Almighty and Eternal Father, since it has pleased Our Divine Saviour to reveal to mankind in modern times the power residing in His Holy Face, we now avail ourselves of this treasure in our great need. Since our Saviour Himself promised that by offering to you His Holy face disfigured in the passion, we can procure the settlement of all the affairs of our household, and that nothing whatsoever will be refused to us, we now come before Your throne.

Eternal Father, turn away Your angry gaze from our guilty people whose face has become unsightly in Your eyes. Look instead upon the Face of Your Beloved Son; for this is the Face of Him in whom you are well pleased. We now offer You His Holy face covered with blood, sweat, dust, spittle and shame, in reparation for the worst crimes of our age, which are atheism, blasphemy and the desecration of Your holy days. We thus hope to appease Your anger justly provoked against us. The All-Merciful Advocate opens His mouth to plead our cause; listen to His cries, behold His tears, O God, and through the merits of His Holy Face, hearken to Him when he intercedes for us poor, miserable sinners. Amen.

Prayer for Church and Country

Holy Father, guard the Church of Jesus Christ in virtue of thy salutary Name, for this was the last will of thy Divine Son, his last desire. Remember the last loving prayer he offered for our holy Mother the Church, Holy Father, keep in thy Name those whom thou hast given me; while I was with them I kept them in thy Name. Most Holy Name of God, refuge of the Church and of (France), have pity on us and save us.

Prayer revealed to Sr. Marie de Saint Pierre (Life of Sister Mary of Saint Peter Carmelite of Tours by M Labbe Janvier.

(Instead of France, you may insert the name of the country which you wish to pray for.)

Holy Face Prayers for the Holy Souls in Purgatory

By a Rescript dated 27th of January 1853. His Holiness Pope Pius IX grants to all who recite, with a contrite heart, these prayers in honour of the Face of Jesus Christ an indulgence of a hundred days for each time applicable to the souls in Purgatory.

Prayer I

I salute Thee, I adore Thee, and I love Thee. O Jesus, my Savior, outraged anew by blasphemers, and I offer Thee, through the heart of Thy blessed Mother, the worship of all the angels, and saints, as an incense and a perfume of sweet odor, most humbly beseeching Thee, by the virtue of Thy Sacred Face, to repair and renew in me and in all men Thy image disfigured by sin. Amen.

Pater, Ave, Gloria (Say one Our Father, one Hail Mary, one Glory Be)

Prayer II

I salute Thee, I adore Thee, and I love Thee. O adorable Face of Jesus, my Beloved, Noble Seal of the Divinity; with all the powers of my soul I apply myself to Thee, and most humbly pray Thee to imprint in us all the features of Thy Divine likeness. Amen.

Prayer III

O adorable Face of my Jesus, so mercifully bowed down upon the tree of the Cross, on the day of Thy Passion for the salvation of men, now again, incline in Thy Pity towards us poor sinners; cast upon us a look of compassion and receive us to the kiss of peace. Amen.

Sacred Heart of Jesus, have mercy on us. Amen.

Sit nomen Domini benedictum! Amen.

Act of Admiration When
Contemplating the Holy Face

O Lord! wherefore hast Thou given us an imprint of Thy Holy Face, in the sad and pitiful state of Thy Passion? Why didst Thou not rather portray it with those sweet traits which enrapture all hearts, or with the dazzling splendour with which it was clothed on the day of Thy glorious Transfiguration?

It seems to me as though Thy admirable beauty would have caused us to feel more delight in Thee and more love for Thee, and all that the majesty of Thy Face would have inspired in us with more reverence! Would not Thy august brow have worn a more gracious aspect, if it had been adorned with a crown of light, or with a diadem, than with only a circlet bristling with thorns?

But no, divine Saviour! Thy Face in its dazzling glory is reserved to be forever the object of the joy of the blessed in Paradise, but Thou ought to be the ordinary subject of our veneration here below, and the model for our imitation. We shall every day experience that nothing is more efficacious for enkindling Thy love in our hearts, for animating us to the practice of all kinds of virtues and for making us avoid sin.

Grant us then the grace, O amiable Saviour, so to compassionate Thy sufferings upon earth, that we may hereafter merit to participate in Thy triumph in heaven. Amen.

Cry of Love

Pardon, pardon, O my God, for the innumerable souls which are being lost, every day, around us. The devil rushes forth from the abyss, hurrying to make horrible conquests; he excites the infernal band; he exclaims: Souls, souls! Let us hasten to ruin souls! — And souls fall like autumn leaves into the eternal abyss. We also, O my God, we will cry: Souls! Souls!

We must have souls wherewith to acquit the debt of gratitude we have contracted towards Thee; we ask them of Thee by the wounds of Jesus, our Saviour. These adorable wounds cry out to Thee even as so many powerful mouths. The King crowned with thorns demands subjects torn from the devil; we ask them from Thee, together with him and by him, for Thy greater glory, and by the intercession of the most holy Virgin Mary, conceived without sin. Amen.

Wine of Mercy Prayer

" Eternal Father, behold the Divine Heart of Jesus, which I now offer thee, wherein to receive the wine of thy justice that it may be changed for us into the wine of mercy"

He gave me to understand that each time I made this offering, a drop of the wine of divine anger would fall into the Sacred Heart of Jesus, and there would be transformed into mercy. "I beg of you, my good mother, to prevail on our sisters to make this offering frequently, for alas! What am I but a miserable atom, incapable of arresting the anger of God?" Life of Sr Mary of Saint Peter by Labbe Janvier 1884 page 288

An Alternate translation/version of this Prayer from the Golden Arrow page 179 is as follows:

"Eternal Father, look upon the Sacred Heart of Jesus, which I offer to you as a Vase that it might receive the wine of Your Justice, and in passing through this Holy Channel that it may be changed for us into the Wine of Your Mercy!

Salutation to Our Lord Jesus Christ

(In Order to Repair the Blasphemies Committed Against His Sacred Name)

In union with the whole Church, by the hearts of Mary and of Joseph all burning with love, and in the name of all men, I salute Thee, I adore Thee, and I love Thee, O Jesus of Nazareth! King of the Jews, full of meekness and of humility, of grace and of truth. Mercy and justice are with Thee; love is Thy substance; Thou art the Christ, the only Son of the living God, and the blessed fruit of the womb of the glorious Virgin Mary.

O Jesus! Good Shepherd, who hast given Thy life for Thy sheep, by all Thy sacred wounds, Thy precious blood, Thy divine tears and beloved sweat, by all the sighs, the groans, the sorrows, the love, the merits of the thirty three years of Thy holy life, enclosed in the ineffable sanctuary of Thy most loving Heart, have pity on us, poor and miserable sinners; convert all the blasphemers and profaners of the holy day of Sunday, and give us a share in Thy divine merits, now and at the hour of our death. Amen.

(This salutation must be repeated three times in order to honour his divine life, his glorious life and his mortal life.)

Aspirations

Eternal Father, I offer Thee the body and blood of our Lord Jesus Christ, in expiation for our sins and for the needs of Holy Church.

Amiable Heart of Jesus, our mediator, appease Thy Father, and save sinners. Powerful heart of Mary, refuge of sinners, stay the arrows of divine justice.

Saint Michael, pray for us.

Saint Martin, pray for us.

Saint Louis, pray for us.

O God our Protector, behold us and cast

Thine eyes upon the Face of Thy Christ. (Ps 83:9.)

Aspirations

Eternal Father, we offer Thee the adorable Face of thy well-beloved Son for the honour and glory of Thy Holy Name and for the salvation of all men. (*Sister Marie de Saint-Pierre.*)

Aspirations During the Day

O adorable Face of Jesus, be the joy of my soul.

O holy Face of Jesus, be the light of my mind.

O adorable Face of Jesus, be the strength of my will.

O adorable Face of Jesus, be the fire of my heart.

O adorable Face of Jesus, be the purity of my body.

O adorable Face of Jesus, be the wisdom of my words.

O adorable Face of Jesus, be the zeal of my apostolate.

O adorable Face of Jesus, be my heaven on earth.

Prayer to the Eternal Father

O almighty and eternal God, it is by the Heart of Jesus, Thy divine Son, my way, my truth and my life, that I draw near to Thee. I come, through this adorable Heart, in union with the holy angels, and with all the Saints, to praise, bless, adore and glorify Thy holy Name, despised and blasphemed by so great a number of sinners.

Accompanied by my desires, the blessed Spirits, ministers of Thy mercy, I go all over the world in order to seek souls bought by the blood of Thy only Son. I offer them all to Thee by the hands of the holy Virgin and of glorious Saint Joseph, under the protection of the angels and of all the Saints, begging of Thee, in the Name and through the merits of Jesus our Saviour, to convert all blasphemers and all who profane the holy day of Sunday, in order that we may all with one voice, one soul and one heart, praise, bless, love, adore and glorify Thy holy Name, in the heights, the depths, the breadths, the immensity, the fullness of the honour, the praise and the infinite adorations that the sacred Heart of Thy well beloved Son renders to Thee; that Heart which is the organ and the delight of the most Holy Trinity, and which alone knows and perfectly adores Thy holy Name in spirit and in truth. Amen.

Prayer to Reproduce the
Image of God in Our Souls

I salute You, I adore You, and I love You, oh adorable Face of my Beloved Jesus, as the noble stamp of the Divinity! Completely surrendering my soul to You, I most humbly beg You to stamp this seal upon us all, so that the Image of God may once more be reproduced by its imprint in our souls. Amen.

Benediction of St. Francis of Assisi
through the Holy Face

The Lord bless thee, and keep thee;

The Lord show his Face to thee, and have mercy on thee;

The Lord turn his countenance towards thee, and give thee peace.

Appendix VI:
Novena to the Holy Face

FIRST DAY: THE HOLY FACE AT BETHLEHEM

Lord, I desire to seek Thy Face; do not Thou repel me far from it on account of my sins; do not remove Thy Holy Spirit from me. Let the light of Thy Face shine upon me; teach me in the way of Thy commandments.

Enter into the grotto at Bethlehem, consider the newborn Child, laid in the cradle, wrapped in poor swaddling clothes. Mary and Joseph stand before Him and contemplate Him. You also gaze upon His sweet and radiant Face. It is the Face of the Emmanuel, of the Son of "God with us "; of the "most beautiful of the children of men". During four thousand years, the patriarchs and prophets had desired to see It; they earnestly entreated for It as the "salvation" promised to the world.

"Lord," they unceasingly exclaimed, "show us Thy Face, and we shall be saved. Behold It here! It shows itself at last! See how ravishing and amiable It is; how It already hastens to give you all the most precious things that It possesses".

I. *It gives you Its first prayer* — Already in Its cradle, It turns towards Heaven; towards the sovereign Father of angels and of men; the Author of all things. It adores Him in your name, It prays for you. "Behold Me," It says, "Oh My Father, I come to fulfill Thy will." Now, this will is to deliver you from eternal death and to accomplish your salvation. When allowing itself to be seen for the first time, the Face of Jesus is humble and suppliant; associate yourself with His prayer; determine to labour efficaciously for the great affair of your salvation, which is the object of His coming.

II. *It gives you Its first tears* — Behold the innocent and delicate cheeks of the newborn Infant benumbed with cold, bathed with the tears which are caused less by the sufferings of the body, than by the grief excited in His soul by the sight of the world. The sweet Face of the little Child Jesus is already the victim of reparation, of justice, and of expiation; It suffers, It weeps, it satisfies for your sins. Gather up with reverence these holy tears, one alone of which possesses infinite value; offer them to the Eternal Father for the payment of your debts towards Him.

III. *It gives you also one of Its first smiles* — It has already smiled on Mary, It has smiled on Joseph; now from out the midst of Its swaddling clothes, from out Its tears, It turns towards you, It becomes sweetly radiant whilst looking at you, It gives you Its infantine smile; a smile of peace and love, a smile of heaven, which invites you, which calls you, which seems to say to you: "*The Face which smiles on you is that of a friend, of a brother, of a Savior. Draw near, have confidence, I love you.*"

Act of love— If the Child Jesus loves you, if his Holy Face gives you the proof of it, what is it that holds you back? Render to Him love for love.

Virtue to be practiced— Detach yourself, at least in heart, from all earthly things; let Jesus be your treasure!

Spiritual bouquet— Dry that first tear; carry away with you that first kind smile of the Holy Face, lay it in the deepest part of your soul, as a ray of hope, as a spark of love, and say with the prophet: "The light of Thy Face has been shed upon us, oh Lord; Thou hast given joy to our heart."

I have called upon Thy Face with my whole heart; have pity on me according to Thy promises. Let the light of Thy Face shine upon me. Save me in Thy mercy, Lord; I shall not be confounded because I have called upon Thee.

PRAYER — God all-powerful and merciful, grant we entreat Thee, that, venerating the Face of Thy Christ, disfigured in His Passion because of our sins, we may deserve to contemplate It eternally in the splendour of the glory of Heaven. Through the same Jesus Christ. Amen.

SECOND DAY: THE HOLY FACE IN
THE MIDST OF THE PEOPLE OF JUDEA

Lord, I desire to seek Thy Face; do not Thou repel me far from It on account of my sins; do not remove Thy Holy Spirit from me. Let the light of Thy Face shine upon me; teach me in the way of Thy commandments.

Follow our Lord during His public life, traversing the towns and villages of Judea, announcing the good tidings of the Gospel, curing sicknesses and infirmities, everywhere as He passed, doing good. Observe what part the Holy Face took in this mission of teaching and of charity. As the Son of God had really united the whole of our nature to Himself, He showed Himself to men, with a human face, having its own individual features, and a physiognomy which caused Him, at all times and everywhere to be known by the aspect of His countenance; for "man", says the prophet, "is known by the aspect of his face." The people strove with all their might to see the Face of Jesus.

Admire the three wonders of grace, which the sight of the adorable Face produced upon all those who drew nigh to It.

I. *It ravished the multitude* — When Jesus appeared in public, the people surrounded Him, eager to see and hear Him; suspended on His divine lips, they said: "Never man spoke like this man!" And they were plunged into ecstasy and astonishment. The reason is that, very different from Moses, the Man-God did not cover His Face with a veil; He revealed Himself to every eye; He conversed with all indiscriminately, tempering, through the sweetness and charm of His humanity, the too dazzling rays of the divinity which dwelt corporeally in Him. His Face was really the mirror of His soul, the outward expression of His heart, the visible manifestation of His internal feelings.

Is it surprising that His aspect ravished all beholders? — Come you also near, contemplate with avidity His Face at once human and divine, listen with reverence to the words of His mouth; delight to listen to It, to question It, to converse with It.

II. *It attracts the apostles* — On a certain day, the Saviour passed near to a publican seated at his desk: "Follow me," He said, and the man immediately arose and followed Him; he became one of His apostles and His first evangelist. "It was," says St. Jerome, "because at the same time that Matthew heard the voice of Jesus, he saw on His Face a ray of divine Majesty which enlightened him and stirred the very depths of his soul." — On another occasion, Andrew brought him his brother. Jesus, casting a penetrating glance upon him, said: "*Thou shalt be called Peter.*" He transformed him and made of him the chief of his apostles, the cornerstone of his Church. — Walking beside the lake, He perceives two fishermen, two brothers, who were mending their nets; He stops, looks at them: "Follow me," He says. On hearing the imperative command and on beholding the splendour which illuminated the eyes and the Face of Him who called to them, they abandon their nets, their bark, their father, and immediately follow Him. Are there not moments in which the Holy Face enlightens you, urges you, and touches you? Do not make any resistance or delay when you are thus attracted by it; let it work in you the change which it desires to do.

III. *It is compassionate and merciful towards all.* Little children are the object of Its embraces and Its caresses. It gives the prodigal son the kiss of peace and reconciliation. Inclined towards the ground in the presence of the repentant sinner, It is raised again in order to look at her and to say: "Go in peace, and sin no more." Attentive to the needs of the multitude in the desert, It raises Its eyes towards heaven and calls down the blessing which multiplies the bread necessary for the subsistence of the hungry people. It sheds tears over the tomb of Lazarus and communicates to the four-day corpse a miraculous resurrection, an image of the possible conversion of the most hardened sinner. Light, grace, pardon, life, flow like rays from the adorable Face; gather them up with avidity

182

according to the needs and the different states of your soul.

Act of confidence— Everywhere that It showed itself upon earth, the Holy Face blessed, pardoned, cured, did good. I will call upon It; wherefore should I not be heard?

Virtue to be practiced— Be docile to the impressions of grace; a grace is a glance of the Face of Jesus which solicits and urges you. Give yourself up to Its heavenly influence.

Spiritual Bouquet— My beloved, show me Thy Face; make Thy voice resound in my ears; Thy voice is as sweet as Thy Face is lovely; I desire at the same time to see and to hear Thee.

I have called upon Thy Face with my whole heart; have pity on me according to Thy promises. Let the light of Thy Face shine upon me. Save me in Thy mercy, Lord; I shall not be confounded because I have called upon Thee.

PRAYER — God all-powerful and merciful, grant we entreat Thee, that, venerating the Face of Thy Christ, disfigured in His Passion because of our sins, we may deserve to contemplate It eternally in the splendour of the glory of Heaven. Through the same Jesus Christ. Amen.

THIRD DAY: THE HOLY FACE ON TABOR

Lord, I desire to seek Thy Face; do not Thou repel me far from It on account of my sins; do not remove Thy Holy Spirit from me. Let the light of Thy Face shine upon me; teach me in the way of Thy commandments.

Ascend with our Lord on Tabor. He climbed the mountain with three privileged disciples, Peter, James, and John, and He began to pray. Whilst He prayed, His Face was transfigured before them; His Holy Face became resplendent like the sun; His vestments were white as snow. Jesus willed to give in this manner a free outlet to the rays of the Divinity which was hidden in Him; for the first time, He caused to appear before mortal eyes His adorable Face with the splendour of the glory and the beauty which belong to It. You will find in this mystery three subjects worthy of your attention:

I. *A spectacle to contemplate* — that of the Face of our Lord beaming with splendour and grace. The light which flows from His divine Face communicates to the raiment of the Saviour and to the whole of His person a virginal whiteness, incomparable in its purity. It is a light which casts Its beams into the air, envelopes the whole mountain, and ravishes the three disciples who are present, with admiration. They experience an ecstasy of happiness, a foretaste of the happiness of heaven, and

Saint Peter exclaims, "It is good for us to be here, let us make three tabernacles!" And yet it was only a passing ray of the eternal splendour, a drop of that ocean of felicity, of that plenitude of life of which the Face of the Lord is the source. What will it be when you drink It in copious drafts and when you will have full possession and assured enjoyment of the very source itself?

II. *A conversation to which to listen* — Listen to the conversation which Moses and Elias have with Jesus in the presence of the Holy Face thus transfigured. — The subject which occupies them is the work of the Redemption of the human race, which the Son of Man has come to accomplish; they speak of His "going out of the world", that is to say, of His Passion and death. The Face of the Redeemer, at that moment so radiant and so beautiful, will soon be wounded, bleeding, spit upon, outraged in a thousand ways. Lifted up upon an infamous gibbet, it will utter in the face of heaven a cry of pardon when expiring, and it will be the consummation of our salvation, the conquering signal of peace, the warrant of an entire reconciliation between God and man. In this mysterious conversation, the Face of Jesus offers Itself to us under two very different aspects; It is at once the glorious and the sorrowful Face. Tabor and Calvary approach each other and are united together; it was meet that it should be so; it is on Calvary, upon the Cross, by the sufferings and ignominy of the

Passion concentrated in the Face of our Lord, that Redemption will be accomplished and that we shall merit together with the beatific vision, the delights of Paradise. Do not separate the idea of the sacrifice from that of the recompense; if the joys of Tabor are sometimes granted you, remember that it is to give you strength, the better to follow Jesus to Calvary, and to bear the Cross with Him.

III. *An order to receive* — This order emanates from the Eternal Father, who, from the summit of the mountain, as from an awe-inspiring tribune, desires to render, in the face of heaven and earth, a solemn homage to the Face of His Son. It is in fact the splendour of His glory, the figure of His substance, the most pure splendour of His eternal light, the spotless mirror of His justice and of His infinite perfections. He there enhances Its glory, by surrounding It as in a splendid frame, with a luminous cloud, which comes down from heaven, as the symbol of the Holy Spirit, from out the bosom of which issues a voice full of power and majesty: *"This is My beloved Son in whom I am well pleased, hear ye Him."* Such is the command which God gives to every creature. He glorifies the Face of His Word, He makes a solemn exposition of It on the highest mountain of the Holy Land, in order to show in It, to all people and to all centuries, the sign of salvation and the organ of truth. Look at It then, "and act according to the model which is presented to you on the mountain."

Act of hope— Yes, I know it; my Redeemer is living. I shall see Him one day with my eyes, in His glory, myself and not another; this is the hope which is laid up in my bosom.

Virtue to be practiced— Fidelity in obeying the divine commandments. "Speak, Lord, Thy servant harkens."

Spiritual bouquet— "It is good for us to be here." Say these words in the presence of the Tabernacle, at the foot of the altar; there is your Tabor, for the immortal and glorious Face of Jesus is, through the Eucharist, present to the eyes of your faith; make It the object of your delights and of your joys.

I have called upon Thy Face with my whole heart; have pity on me according to Thy promises. Let the light of Thy Face shine upon me. Save me in Thy mercy, Lord, I shall not be confounded because I have called upon Thee.

PRAYER — God all-powerful and merciful, grant we entreat Thee, that, venerating the Face of Thy Christ, disfigured in His Passion because of our sins, we may deserve to contemplate It eternally in the splendour of the glory of Heaven. Through the same Jesus Christ. Amen.

FOURTH DAY: THE HOLY FACE
IN THE GARDEN OF OLIVES

Lord, I desire to seek Thy Face; do not Thou repel me far from It on account of my sins; do not remove Thy Holy Spirit from me. Let the light of Thy Face shine upon me; teach me in the way of Thy commandments.

Follow Jesus, going after the last supper to the Mount of Olives, in order to prepare Himself for His Passion. He kneels down apart in a solitary grotto; He prays for a long time, even for three hours. His soul is a prey to sorrow, to fear, to the anguish of death. From time to time, He interrupts His prayer in order to go to His disciples and to seek from them a little support and consolation, and He meets with neither. "I have sought," He says, "someone who would console Me, and I have found none." You may here observe three things:

I. *The sorrowful state of the Holy Face* — It reflects all the impressions of His soul; It is sorrowful, desolate, quivering; It sheds tears; sorrowful sighs escape from Its lips. See also, how, after having prayed on His knees, the Saviour, in order to give to His petitions more of intensity and fervour, prostrates Himself with His Face to the ground. Contemplate His Divine Face abased to the dust, cleaving to the earth which, cursed through the sin of Adam and condemned to produce nothing but thorns,

188

was purified by the kiss of peace, by the tears of the Holy Face. Our earth will henceforth behold its inhabitants produce a rich harvest of flowers and fruits of virtue, but Jesus takes the thorns for Himself and with them crowns His brow.

II. *The apparition of the angel* — At that moment, the anguish of the Man-God is redoubled; He experiences mortal anguish; a mysterious sweat, a sweat of blood, bathes His Face, runs down from His brow and falls, drop after drop, upon the ground where He is prostrated. An angel appears in order to strengthen Him; reanimated by the heavenly aid, Jesus rises, accepts the chalice offered to Him by His Father and lovingly drinks it down to the very dregs. Angel of consolation, you give me an example; I envy you your destiny; I desire to put myself in your place; let it be my portion to raise that suffering and languishing Face, to compensate It by the tenderness of my love, and the generosity of my sacrifices; since it is for me that It suffers and that It is humiliated; it is for me that It resigns itself to drink the chalice presented to It by Its Father.

III. *What you have to do* — It is to offer yourself to It and to imitate It. Adorable Face, Thou didst not refuse the succour offered by another and the consolation of an angel. Permit me, in spite of my unworthiness, to draw nigh to Thee, and to render Thee the like service. Permit me to compassionate Thy sorrow, to raise Thee from the ground and to hold Thee reverently in my arms. It is for me to prostrate myself to the ground, to annihilate myself in a spirit of reparation; I associate myself with Thy humiliations and Thy sufferings; like Thee, I accept the chalice of suffering, and I give myself up to the divine will, saying: "Behold me, Lord, I come to do Thy will. Thy law shall be engraved forever in my heart. Thy will and not my own be done; not what I will, oh Lord, but what Thou willest!"

Act of abandonment — Offer yourself wholly to God in order never to do aught save His adorable will; make the offering in union with Jesus praying in the garden.

Virtue to be practiced — Do penance; excite yourself to contrition for your own sins and for those of others; accept, in a spirit of expiation, the trials of life and the bitter sorrows it may please God to send you.

Spiritual bouquet — My food, that is to say, my joy and my delight, are to do the will of my Father who is in heaven.

I have called upon Thy Face with my whole heart; have pity on me according to Thy promises. Let the light of Thy Face shine upon me. Save me in Thy mercy, Lord, I shall not be confounded because I have called upon Thee.

PRAYER — God all-powerful and merciful, grant we entreat Thee, that, venerating the Face of Thy Christ, disfigured in His Passion because of our sins, we may deserve to contemplate It eternally in the splendour of the glory of Heaven. Through the same Jesus Christ. Amen.

FIFTH DAY: THE HOLY FACE
IN THE HOUSE OF CAIPHAS

Lord, I desire to seek Thy Face; do not Thou repel me far from It on account of my sins; do not remove Thy Holy Spirit from me. Let the light of Thy Face shine upon me; teach me in the way of Thy commandments.

It is the night of the Passion. Jesus, after a decisive judgment, has been disdainfully sent, with His hands tied, to the house of Caiphas.

I. *Outrages* — He is at the mercy of a band of servants and of soldiers, who make it a cruel sport to load Him with outrages and insults of every kind. His Holy Face is their target. The whole night, It has to suffer the most humiliating insults which can be invented by the malice of men and the rage of devils. They outrage Him by blows, they wound Him and cover Him with blood by giving Him cuffs with their hands, they soil Him with spits, a kind of insult particularly felt by the Saviour. He complains of it by the mouth of the prophet: *"They were not afraid to spit in My Face,"* and when predicting to His apostles the Passion which He was about to undergo at Jerusalem, He specified the spits which would be given Him: *"The Son of man shall be spit upon."*

II. *Conversion of Saint Peter* — In the midst of this ignominious treatment, what patience on the part of the Saviour! What serenity! What sweetness! He does not complain, He does not murmur; He prays, He loves, He expiates and repairs the outrages which our sins have inflicted and still inflict on the majesty of His heavenly Father. At the very culmination of His ignominies, His sorrowful Face finds means to perform an act of mercy and of ineffable charity; It casts Its eyes on the prince of the apostles and raises him up after his fall. Peter was there, at some distance from Him, an unfaithful disciple, mingling in the crowd of the enemies of His master, he had shamefully denied Him, no less than three times. All at once, he encounters the Divine eyes fixing upon him a look of gentle reproach, of compassion, and of love. It is enough. The sight of that sorrowful Face, of that ray of light which issues from those sad eyes, pierces the heart of the apostle; penetrated with shame and repentance, he turns aside and weeps bitterly.

III. *Application to yourself* — Oh Divine Face who raises up and transforms wandering souls, cast Thine eyes upon me, have pity on me, I have not, after having offended God, responded to the attractions of Thy grace, or, if I have shed a few tears, they have only been the result of a passing feeling of humility, of a sadness in which self-love had a larger part than true repentance. Since Thou art, O adorable Face, a sun of justice, able to soften our souls and to purify our consciences, burn and consume in me all that is contrary to the purity of Thy love; may Thy heavenly rays inflame me, and make me weep secretly over my past offenses; I also am an unfaithful disciple, or rather, I have been, but will no longer be one! Thou hast been so merciful as to forgive me my revolts and to turn away Thine eyes from my sins. No, my Jesus, whatever may happen, and whatever it may cost me, I will not renounce Thee anymore; I will, on the contrary, glorify Thee by my penitence and my good works.

Act of contrition — Lord, turn away Thy Face from my sins and blot out all my iniquities. I detest them and desire to make reparation for them.

Virtue to be practiced — Have the courage of your faith, do not fear the eyes and the words of men, when there is a question of a duty to be fulfilled or of a fault to be avoided.

Spiritual bouquet — Jesus looked at Peter, and Peter wept bitterly.

I have called upon Thy Face with my whole heart; have pity on me according to Thy promises. Let the light of Thy Face shine upon me. Save me in Thy mercy, Lord, I shall not be confounded because I have called upon Thee.

PRAYER — God all-powerful and merciful, grant we entreat Thee, that, venerating the Face of Thy Christ, disfigured in His Passion because of our sins, we may deserve to contemplate It eternally in the splendour of the glory of Heaven. Through the same Jesus Christ. Amen.

SIXTH DAY: THE HOLY FACE AT THE PRAETORIUM OF PILATE

Lord, I desire to seek Thy Face; do not Thou repel me far from It on account of my sins; do not remove Thy Holy Spirit from me. Let the light of Thy Face shine upon me; teach me in the way of Thy commandments.

I. *The sufferings of the Holy Face* — The lashes which the executioners inflicted on Jesus did not spare His sweet and amiable Face. It is furrowed in every direction, wounded, bleeding, lacerated by scourges. Then, seeing that Jesus was condemned to death because

194

He had called himself "King", the soldiers turned this title into a subject of bitter derision and of sacrilegious mockeries. They cast upon His shoulders a purple robe; instead of a sceptre, they place a reed in His hand, and by an incredible refinement of malice, they fashion a crown for Him out of thorns which they interlace together, and which they fasten on His brow with great blows. The long, hard, sharp thorns entering deeply into the head of the Saviour caused Him dreadful suffering and inundated His Holy Face with streams of blood.

II. *Humiliations of the Holy Face* — It was in this pitiable state that Pilate presented Jesus to the people, hoping thereby to excite their compassion and to deliver Him. "Behold the man!" he said. The sight only inflamed their fury. "Crucify him, crucify him, they exclaimed. — Shall I crucify your king? — We have no other king than Cesar, we will not have this man to reign over us."The enemies of the Saviour triumphed. Amongst the crowd, there were many whom He had overwhelmed with blessings, who perhaps, in secret, called themselves His disciples and friends; yet not one amongst them raised his voice in order to declare himself in His favour, and to defend Him; not one of them dared to recognize Him for his king and his God. This miserable, cowardly abandonment, joined to the other outrages inflicted on the Holy Face, was a sorrowful martyrdom for Jesus. *"My people, what have I done to you? Why do you outrage the*

Face of your Saviour? Why have you surrounded it with a diadem of thorns?"

III. *Honour due to the Holy Face* — There is a profound mystery contained in the crowning of the divine Face; it was destined to reign. The soldiers, though unconscious of it, attest the royalty of Jesus Christ, as well as Pilate; without being aware of it, they enter into the designs of God, who wills that His Son should be recognized as King and under that title, should receive the homage of all creatures. — Yes, Oh Jesus, by the diadem which crowns Thy Face, Thou hast acquired the right of reigning over my heart; Thy diadem of ignominy and of suffering is a crown of expiation and of love. Many times I have cast dishonor upon Thy royalty by despising Thy holy law and Thy divine teachings; many times I have caused the blood to flow down Thy august Face through my reiterated sins, which have driven ever deeper into Thy flesh the thorns which transpierce Thy brow; I have run after the joys of this world, and I have crowned myself with roses; I have longed after the luxurious delights of an easy and pleasant life, not remembering that I am the subject of a King crowned with thorns.

No, adorable Face, I will not allow Thee any more to suffer the thorns of my iniquities; I desire that Thou shouldst rejoice in my homage; that thou shouldst be crowned with flowers of my virtues, and that Thou shouldst triumph in me by a generous love worthy of Thee.

Act of offering — Oh Jesus, my king, and my God, behold my mind with its thoughts, my heart with its affections, my will with its tendencies, behold my soul and my body; I put them wholly and entirely under the empire of Thy Holy Face, reign over me forevermore.

Virtue to be practiced— Make all the desires and ill-regulated movements of your heart and mind which may offend the Holy Face and renew Its sufferings, to die in you by means of mortification.

Spiritual bouquet — Can a member be fastidious and sensual under a Head that is crowned with thorns?

I have called upon Thy Face with my whole heart; have pity on me according to Thy promises. Let the light of Thy Face shine upon me. Save me in Thy mercy, Lord; I shall not be confounded because I have called upon Thee.

PRAYER — God all-powerful and merciful, grant we entreat Thee, that, venerating the Face of Thy Christ, disfigured in His Passion because of our sins, we may deserve to contemplate It eternally in the splendour of the glory of Heaven. Through the same Jesus Christ. Amen.

SEVENTH DAY: THE HOLY FACE
ON THE PATH TO CALVARY

Lord, I desire to seek Thy Face; do not Thou repel me far from It on account of my sins; do not remove Thy Holy Spirit from me. Let the light of Thy Face shine upon me; teach me in the way of Thy commandments.

Behold Jesus ascending the mount of His sacrifice, laden with the weight of His Cross. After the painful and humiliating fall which He has had, His adorable Face is soiled with dust, with sweat and with blood. The spectacle excites the contempt of the crowd and the mockeries of the executioners.

I. *Reparation offered to the Holy Face* — In this state of abandonment and of opprobrium, the Saviour, all at once, receives a mark of devotion and of tenderness which compensates and consoles Him. A courageous woman, Veronica, has been touched with compassion. Listening only to her faith and her love, she makes her way through the crowd, puts aside the executioners, and, filled with reverence and emotion, draws near to Jesus. Then she takes the soft white veil of fine Egyptian linen which covers her head; she spreads it over and gently applies it to the bleeding and wounded Face of the Man-God! She wipes It and raises It; it is a real service which she renders to Him, and which for a moment relieves His sufferings and reanimates Him. As a recompense, Jesus immediately leaves the impression of His Holy Face upon the linen of which she had made use for the performance of this heroic act.

II. *Veronica, our pattern* — Congratulate Veronica; look upon her as an admirable model, learn from that generous woman to make reparation to the suffering Face of your God. Impiety renews, in these our days, the outrages He endured on Calvary. His Holy Face is especially insulted and spat upon by all the horrible blasphemies which hell vomits forth against His divinity. The Saviour complains; He seems to say to those who know Him and who love Him: "*I have sought around Me for consolers, and I have found none.*" Let your heart answer: "Behold me, Lord; I am Thine, ready to do Thy good pleasure. Must I oppose my faith, my adoration, my example to hatred and contemptuous impiety? I am ready."

III. *A good inspiration to follow* — Divine Master, Thou hast said in Thy Gospel: "*Whoever shall glorify Me before man, I will glorify him in My turn before My Father who is in heaven.*" At the present day, perverse and sacrilegious sects outrage Thy adorable Face; I desire to glorify It by my expiations, by my praises, by all the fervour of my love. Animate me with the spirit with which Veronica was inspired upon the ascent to Calvary.

What signifies to me the raillery of the world, and the rage of hell? I will listen to the voice of the Church, I will follow the inspirations of my heart, I will go to Thee, oh sweet Face of my Savior; I will wipe away the tears with which It is inundated; I will soothe the wounds which make It suffer, I will efface the ignominious blemishes with which wicked men have attempted to soil It. In Thy turn, inspire me with the rays of Thy grace, and engrave in my heart the celestial impress of Thy virtues.

Act of charity— Love the Holy Face and have compassion on the outrages It was made to suffer; love your wandering brethren and pray to God to spare and convert them.

Virtue to be practiced— Let zeal for reparation inflame you; exercise it by communions, by your prayers, by your words, by your example, by all the means with which the sight of evil committed ought to inspire you.

Spiritual bouquet— "*I want Veronicas,*" said our Lord to Marie de Saint Pierre. — "*My daughter, take My Face as a precious coin wherewith to pay to My Father the debts of His justice.*"

I have called upon Thy Face with my whole heart; have pity on me according to Thy promises. Let the light of

Thy Face shine upon me. Save me in Thy mercy, Lord, I shall not be confounded because I have called upon Thee.

PRAYER — God all-powerful and merciful, grant we entreat Thee, that, venerating the Face of Thy Christ, disfigured in His Passion because of our sins, we may deserve to contemplate It eternally in the splendour of the glory of Heaven. Through the same Jesus Christ. Amen.

EIGHTH DAY: THE HOLY
FACE ON THE CROSS

Lord, I desire to seek Thy Face; do not Thou repel me far from It on account of my sins; do not remove Thy Holy Spirit from me. Let the light of Thy Face shine upon me; teach me in the way of Thy commandments.

Upon the Cross, where it is placed as upon an altar of propitiation between heaven and earth, the Holy Face acts as our intercessor and our mediator.

I. *The pardon of the Holy Face* — Raising Its eyes bathed in tears towards the heavenly Father, It entreats our pardon: *Pater, dimitte illis.* Oh Father, remit the debt of these sinners; give back to them Thy friendship. Then turning towards us, It inclines Itself lovingly, as though to offer us the kiss of peace and of reconciliation. Oh, how touching, at that moment, is the aspect of the sorrowful Face of the Redeemer; what sufferings upon that bed of anguish! What a prolonged agony! And what patience also! What gentleness, what an ineffable serenity in Its movements and Its words!

As often as seven times, the Divine Face, giving a truce to Its sufferings, opens Its blessed lips; each one of Its words is a lesson, a grace, and as it were, a reiterated and supreme adieu which It addresses to the world. It does not murmur; It is not irritated; It prays, It pardons, It blesses; at last It utters a loud cry and expires.

II. *The appeal made to Divine mercy* — O God, our Creator, and our Father, we dare not raise our eyes towards Thee; for we have sinned; we have abused Thy innumerable blessings; we are guilty in the highest degree, we deserve the blows of Thy divine justice. But, Lord, behold Thy Christ on the Cross, look at His merciful and compassionate Face which implores Thee. Listen to the voice of Its prayer. Behold Its tears, the thorns of Its crown, the blood with which It is inundated. Behold It mute, inanimate, growing cold in the death agony. It is given up to death for us, O Father; It has taken our place before Thee, It has deserved to disarm Thy anger. Look, look at the Face of Thy well-beloved Christ, in the state to which It has been reduced. Pardon us, O most merciful Father, and save us.

III. *Christian pardon* — Most Holy Face of Jesus on the cross, what a lesson Thou gives to me! Thy charity has reached even to the extent of pardoning Thy executioners and praying for them. It is, above all, for those who struck Thee, wounded Thee, and dealt Thee blows, and covered Thee with spittle that Thou said: *"Forgive them, Father, they know not what they do."* When they struck Thee, Thou didst endure them, gently and in silence. Now, Thou raises Thy voice to excuse and defend them, to obtain pardon for them; in offering for them Thy blood, Thou gives them the greatest proof of Thy love. Teach me this Thy endurance of our neighbour and this Thy generosity in pardoning even our most cruel enemies. Yes, I forgive, for love of Thee, all who have offended me. With you, I pray for the sinners who outrage Thee, for the wretched men who blaspheme Thee; I beg of Thee their conversion and their salvation. Let them but turn to Thee, O most Holy Face, let them invoke Thee; it is enough! Whoever looks on Thee, O blessed Face, with faith and repentance, will escape the sting of the serpent and will find life.

Act of generous love — My God, I forget the injuries which have been inflicted on me; I pardon all those who have offended me in any way whatever, I love them sincerely, I pray for them, and I entreat Thee to save them.

Virtue to be practiced — Bear the injuries inflicted on you and the coldness shown you by your neighbour, accept all that is painful in them to your heart and mind in reparation for what the Holy Face has suffered.

Spiritual bouquet — God our protector, cast Thine eyes upon the Face of Thy Christ.

I have called upon Thy Face with my whole heart; have pity on me according to Thy promises. Let the light of Thy Face shine upon me. Save me in Thy mercy, Lord, I shall not be confounded because I have called upon Thee.

PRAYER — God all-powerful and merciful, grant we entreat Thee, that, venerating the Face of Thy Christ, disfigured in His Passion because of our sins, we may deserve to contemplate It eternally in the splendour of the glory of Heaven. Through the same Jesus Christ. Amen.

NINTH DAY: THE HOLY FACE ON THE DAY OF THE RESURRECTION

Lord, I desire to seek Thy Face; do not Thou repel me far from It on account of my sins; do not remove Thy Holy Spirit from me. Let the light of Thy Face shine upon me; teach me in the way of Thy commandments.

On the day of His resurrection, our Saviour showed Himself several times to His holy mother, to the holy women, and to His apostles. He came forth from the sepulchre, endowed with a spiritual and incorruptible life, shining with glory and immortality. In this state, that which above all attracted attention was the beauty and triumphant splendour of His Holy Face.

I. *Glory of the Holy Face after the Resurrection* — Look at It yourself in spirit and with the eyes of faith. What celestial fire in Its eyes! What serenity on Its brow! What harmony in Its features! What a smiling and majestic countenance! During His Passion, we beheld the Face of Jesus bleeding and full of grief; at this moment, joy beams forth from It; It overflows with consolation in proportion to the sufferings and ignominies It has suffered. O, adorable Face of my Saviour, it is meet that victorious now, over death and sin, You should appear dazzling in strength and splendour. Show what Thou art; shed all around in softened majesty, the rays of honour and glory with which Thou art crowned; advance and reign over all hearts. *Prospere procede, et regna.*

II. *Joy which It communicates* — The first time that the apostles, when they were assembled together in the cenacle, saw the risen Face of their divine Master, they were thrilled, says the Evangelist, with great joy; His smile, His sweet gaze, His kind and paternal words, the breath of His lips which He shed upon them, inundated them interiorly with a delicious peace which they had never before experienced. What will be the joy of the elect when they shall behold, in its full splendour, without a cloud, and without a shade, the glorious Face of the Incarnate Word? The sight will enable them to penetrate as through a most pure mirror, into the secrets of the Divine Essence, where they will find perfect beatitude and the sovereign good. They will see It even as It is, that most Holy Face, and they will become like It; perfection of soul and of body will be theirs through the light of Its glory, with which they will feel themselves to be penetrated.

III. *Its praises throughout eternity* — Lord, permit me "to behold Thee", permit me to see Thy Face in Its pure and real glory; when Thy glory shall thus appear to me, then my heart will be satiated with joy. Being then, says Saint Augustine, free and disengaged from all cares, "we shall see, we shall love, we shall praise; " we shall see the Face of the Divine King so ravishing and so beautiful; we shall love the Face of the Man-God, of the Son of Mary so sweet and so amiable; we shall praise the Face of the Redeemer, so victorious and so powerful. We shall behold It forever, we shall love It without distaste; we shall praise It without weariness, with transports of ever reviving, ever renewed joy, forever and ever. Amen.

Act of desire — When shall I go and appear before the Face of my God? When shall I see Him face-to-face?

Virtue to be practiced — Detach yourself, little by little, from the deceptive and passing joys of this world; seek the treasures of Heaven where the risen Jesus awaits you.

Spiritual bouquet — May I expire thirsting with an ardent thirst to see the desirable Face of our Lord, Jesus Christ. (Last words of Mr. Dupont)

I have entreated Thy Face with my whole heart; have pity on me according to Thy promise. Make the light of Thy Face to shine upon me; save me in Thy mercy; Lord, I shall not be confounded, because I have called upon Thee.

PRAYER — Almighty and merciful God, grant, we beg of Thee, that whilst venerating the Face of Thy Christ, disfigured in the Passion because of our sins, we may merit to contemplate It eternally in the splendour of Its heavenly glory. Through the same Jesus Christ our Lord. Amen.

Concluding Word

Sent from Lisieux

At the heart of this little way shines the Holy Face of Christ. It is a Face marred by suffering yet radiant with love, a silent Gospel that invites us to trust, to offer, to surrender. St. Thérèse teaches us that sanctity does not lie in great deeds but in small acts of love performed with great fidelity. And Fulton Sheen reminds us that in contemplating the Holy Face, every tear, every sacrifice, every hidden offering becomes a seed of redemption.

As you close these pages, may you open your heart to the Face of Jesus, and through daily fidelity to love, allow Him to engrave His likeness upon your soul. The world awaits saints made luminous by His countenance. Let us go forth, then, carrying the imprint of His Face, and living the Little Way of trust and surrender.

About the Author

Allan Smith is a Catholic evangelist, radio host, and spiritual director who has spent over a decade proclaiming the wisdom of Archbishop Fulton J. Sheen to audiences around the world. As the founder of Bishop Sheen Today, Al has edited and published dozens of classic Sheen titles, including 'The Cries of Jesus from the Cross' and 'Lord, Teach Us to Pray'.

A passionate promoter of Eucharistic Reparation and devotion to the Holy Face of Jesus, Al regularly speaks at parish missions, leads retreats, and hosts weekly radio broadcasts across Canada, the United States, Ireland, Australia and the Philippines. His work has helped reintroduce Sheen's powerful spiritual legacy to a new generation.

He lives in Canada with his family and continues his mission of calling souls to deeper intimacy with Christ through the example of saints like St. Thérèse of Lisieux and the timeless teachings of Fulton Sheen.

To learn more or to access free devotional resources, visit our two websites at:

www.bishopsheentoday.com

www.holyfacemiracle.com

About the Sheen Mission Series

The Sheen Mission Series is a four-volume spiritual journey inspired by Archbishop Fulton J. Sheen. Each book is designed as a devotional companion — guiding the faithful in prayer, reparation, and renewal through the Holy Face of Jesus, the Cross, the Eucharist and the maternal love of Our Blessed Mother.

The series can be read in any order, yet together it forms a complete mission of grace:

- **Volume I –** *The Holy Face and the Little Way*
  Walk with St. Thérèse of Lisieux in her Little Way of love, united to the devotion of the Holy Face of Jesus.

- **Volume II –** *Behold Your Mother*
  Enter into Mary's tender care at the foot of the Cross and discover the strength of her Seven Sorrows.

- **Volume III – *The Cross and the Last Words***
  Pray with Archbishop Sheen at Calvary as he opens the treasures of the Seven Last Words of Christ.

- **Volume IV – *Lord, Show Us Thy Face and We Shall Be Saved***
  A mission of light and transformation, centered on the Eucharist and the saving power of Christ's Face.

The Sheen Mission Series invites you to walk with Archbishop Fulton J. Sheen in prayer, reparation, and renewal — a journey of the Holy Face, the Cross, the Eucharist, and Our Blessed Mother.

J M J

A Personal Invitation

Over the years, I have had the privilege of helping souls draw closer to Christ through prayer, silence, and the beautiful wisdom of Archbishop Fulton J. Sheen.

If this devotional has nourished your heart, you may also find these works helpful in your journey of faith:

Advent and Christmas with Archbishop Fulton J. Sheen

- A Devotional Journey of Waiting, Welcoming, and Living the Mystery

Daily readings and gentle reflections to guide the heart from hope to joy — from the quiet longing of Advent to the radiant wonder of Christmas.

Priest, Prophet & King

- Meditations on Identity, Mission, and the Call to Holiness

Reflections on what it means to truly belong to Christ — in our families, vocations, and daily life.

The Sheen Mission Series
Collected Meditations

- Over 100 of the Richest Reflections from Retreats, Radio, and Prayer

A treasury to keep on the nightstand — for those ten-minute moments of quiet that become encounters with God.

May every book you read be an open door to the heart of Christ.

May these works draw you deeper into prayer, trust, peace, and surrender.

And may the Child of Bethlehem be born again in you.

Come, Lord Jesus.

To learn more or to stay connected:
www.bishopsheentoday.com

www.ingramcontent.com/pod-product-compliance
Lightning Source LLC
Chambersburg PA
CBHW060235050426

42448CB00009B/1444